An Introduction to Modern Financial Reporting Theory

Accounting and Finance Series

Consulting editor: Michael Sherer,
University of Essex

The aim of this series is to publish lively and readable textbooks for university students and professionals and up-to-date reference books for researchers, managers and practising accountants. All the authors have been commissioned because of their specialist knowledge of their subjects and their established reputations as lecturers and researchers. Every major topic in accounting and finance will be included, and the series will give special emphasis to recent developments in the field and to issues of continuing debate and controversy. Books in the series include:

An Introduction to Modern Financial Reporting Theory

Brian A. Rutherford

P·C·P
Paul Chapman
Publishing Ltd

To Lynne

Paul Chapman Publishing Ltd
A SAGE Publications Company
6 Bonhill Street
London EC2A 4PU

SAGE Publications Inc.
2455 Teller Road
Thousand Oaks, California 91320

SAGE Publications India Pvt Ltd
32, M-Block Market
Greater Kailash – I
New Delhi 110 048

British Library Cataloguing in Publication data

A catalogue record for this book is available
from the British Library

ISBN 0 7619 6606 4
ISBN 0 7619 6607 2 (pbk)

Library of Congress catalog card number is available

Typeset by Mayhew Typesetting, Rhayader, Powys
Printed and bound in Great Britain by Athenaeum Press, Gateshead

Contents

Series Editor's Preface

It is more than a quarter of a century since the Accounting Standards Steering Committee published The Corporate Report, the first comprehensive attempt to produce a conceptual framework for financial reporting in the UK. Immediately on its publication in 1975, The Corporate Report was embroiled in controversy: it was labelled 'radical', 'unworkable' and accused of 'current cost accounting by the back door'. Perhaps because of the heat of the debate that ensued, The Corporate Report was an essential item on the reading list of all financial reporting courses for countless generations of accounting students in universities and colleges.

The modern equivalent of The Corporate Report is the Accounting Standard Board's Statement of Principles, published in December 1999. It too is a conceptual framework for financial reporting in the UK and it too has generated much controversy. The publication of this book is therefore most welcome, not only for its timeliness but also for the illumination Brian Rutherford brings to the subject. He takes the reader through the Statement of Principles paragraph by paragraph, line by line, and even term by term, so that by the end of the book there is not one part of the Statement that has not been dissected, analysed, interpreted and evaluated.

The thoroughness of the author's review of the Statement of Principles is matched by the clarity of his writing. Although he assumes that the reader will have some prior learning or experience of financial reporting, he knows that he or she will not be steeped in the theoretical foundations of accounting. Rutherford's many years' experience of teaching financial accounting to both university and professional students has enabled him to write this book with them foremost in mind. New concepts and terms are carefully explained and illustrated with both everyday and accounting examples.

The structure of each chapter follows a similar pattern. First, Rutherford presents the outline of the chapter and the fundamental issues to be discussed. Second, he analyses in depth the meaning and interpretation of the relevant paragraphs from the *Statement of Principles*. Third, he offers up the criticisms that have been voiced by both academics and practitioners and subjects them to his own critical evaluation. Finally, he gives copious examples of how the concepts in the Statement of Principles can be applied to the items in the financial statements.

An Introduction to Modern Financial Reporting Theory will undoubtedly become the definitive analytical textbook on the Accounting Standard Board's Statement of Principles for generations of financial reporting students. It is both a pleasure and a privilege to include Brian's book in the Accounting and Finance Series.

Michael Sherer
University of Essex

Preface

In December 1999, the Accounting Standards Board adopted a Statement of Principles for Financial Reporting. Now, for the first time in history, we have an authoritative specification of the conceptual framework which should govern the production of British financial statements. The framework is of direct and practical interest to students of accountancy because it can help to explain why and how financial reporting is carried out, why financial statements are prepared in the way that they are, and why accounting standards specify one method rather than another.

The framework will help students to understand how the methods specified by accounting standards relate to each other and how practice has developed and will continue to develop. They will be able to see the financial reporting curriculum as a coherent whole, rather than a series of discrete and largely unrelated topics, and this will aid learning.

The text of the Accounting Standards Board's Statement is directed at members of the accounting profession engaged in financial reporting and is thus designed to be read by those who are already fully familiar with accounting practice. This book explains the content of the Statement from the perspective of a student of accountancy. It emphasizes and enlarges on the key features of the framework, provides many more examples, shows how the framework applies in practice and also offers some criticisms of its content.

This is a work of accounting theory, in that it describes an abstract system of reasoning to be employed in generating financial reporting numbers. It sets out the system of reasoning that the Accounting Standards Board believes should underlie financial reporting and has said that it will use in developing accounting standards. This is theory of immediate practical relevance to the financial reporting process. The book does not examine alternative possible systems that might be used in financial reporting, or social scientific theories about why accountants behave in the way that they do. These are, of course, enormously interesting and challenging areas, but they lie outside the scope of my text. If this work contributes to readers' understanding of the structure which underlies current financial reporting, it will have achieved its objective.

The theory set out in this book is not, in the main, new. It closely resembles the US standard-setting body's own conceptual framework, which is now getting on for twenty years old, and itself rests on ideas that had been circulating for several decades. What is new, and what makes the theory modern and justifies the use of that term in the title of the book, is its explicit adoption by the body responsible for setting UK accounting standards.

The book begins with a brief examination of the role of financial reporting theory and the emergence of conceptual frameworks. Thereafter, its structure follows that of the Accounting Standards Board's Statement quite closely. The objective of financial statements and the qualitative characteristics which financial information should display are established. From this perspective, the elements which financial statements should contain are then defined. Succeeding chapters look at when and how these elements should be recognized and measured and how the resulting information should be presented. This book's structure departs from that of the Statement in one way. The Statement examines, quite early on, how the entities which should present financial statements should themselves be defined. Although this is the appropriate location in terms of the logic of the model, the material is actually easier to understand once the later stages in the framework have been digested and, in this book, the material comes at the end.

The book is aimed primarily at students on university and professional courses in advanced financial accounting. It will support mainstream textbooks which have space only to give relatively brief coverage of the Statement of Principles and which are not structured in a way that ties the practices described back to their underlying conceptual foundations.

Brian A. Rutherford
Canterbury

Pronouncements Cited

The authoritative pronouncements, exposure drafts and other documents listed are referred to throughout the text by the abbreviations given here.

UK Accounting Standards Board Statement of Principles

SP   Statement of Principles for Financial Reporting (December 1999)
            References to paragraphs in the main text give the chapter and paragraph number (for example, SP, 4.2(a)). References to other parts of the Statement give page number or section title and paragraph number, as appropriate.
SPED 1999   Statement of Principles for Financial Reporting, Revised Exposure Draft (March 1999)

US Financial Accounting Standards Board Statement of Financial Accounting Concepts

SFAC6   Elements of Financial Statements (December 1985)

Financial Reporting Standards

FRS3   Reporting Financial Performance (October 1992)
FRS4   Capital Instruments (December 1993)
FRS5   Reporting the Substance of Transactions (April 1994)
FRS9   Associates and Joint Ventures (November 1997)
FRS10   Goodwill and Intangible Assets (December 1997)
FRS12   Provisions, Contingent Liabilities and Contingent Assets (September 1998)
FRS15   Tangible Fixed Assets (February 1999)

Statements of Standard Accounting Practice

SSAP2   Disclosure of Accounting Policies (November 1971)
SSAP6   Extraordinary Items and Prior Year Adjustments (April 1974) (withdrawn October 1992)
SSAP9   Stocks and Long-Term Contracts (May 1975)
SSAP13   Accounting for Research and Development (December 1977)
SSAP15   Accounting for Deferred Tax (October 1978)
SSAP18   Accounting for Contingencies (August 1980) (withdrawn September 1998)
SSAP21   Accounting for Leases and Hire Purchase Contracts (August 1984)
SSAP25   Segmental Reporting (June 1980)

Financial Reporting Exposure Draft

FRED21   Accounting Policies (December 1999)

Oil Industry Accounting Committee Statement of Recommended Practice

SORP2   Accounting for Oil and Gas Exploration and Development Activities (December 1987)

UK legislation

CA   Companies Act 1985 as amended by the Companies Act 1989

Accounting Standards Committee document

ASC   Foreword to the IASC Framework for the Preparation and Presentation of Financial Statements (1989)

Other Accounting Standards Board documents

SOA   Statement of Aims (1993)
DP   Discussion Paper: *Accounting for Tax* (March 1995)
DP   Discussion Paper: *Derivatives and Other Financial Instruments* (July 1996)
DP   Discussion Paper: *Business Combinations* (December 1998)
DP   Discussion Paper: *Leases: Implementation of a New Approach* (December 1999)

1

The Role of Financial Reporting Theory

It is possible to make a useful working distinction between accounting theories and theories of accounting (see, for example, Most, 1982: Chapter 3). *Accounting theories* are the abstract systems of reasoning to which accountants refer (or could refer) in carrying out their practical work of generating accounting numbers. They can be contrasted with *theories of accounting*, which seek to explain the human activity known as accountancy and which, because accountancy is a human activity, are generally formulated within the domain of the social sciences. We might make a similar distinction between medical theories, that is, the theories drawn from biology, chemistry, and so on which underlie the treatments prescribed by clinicians, and economic and social theories of medical practice formulated to explain, for example, why clinicians might treat similar conditions in different ways depending on how the patient is being funded.

This is a book about accounting theory, and specifically about financial reporting theory, by which we mean those abstract systems of accounting reasoning of relevance to the generation of the accounting numbers reported in financial statements. It is sometimes suggested that there is no need for theory in this area, or even that theory here would be useless or dangerous. After all, surely what accountants are doing is simply measuring concretely occurring events, such as purchases and sales, using common-sense methods, and then reporting their results, using equally common-sense procedures for aggregating and classifying the data?

This argument, however, ignores the widely accepted view that observation of any kind is theory dependent: that is, that theory precedes observation in the sense that, if observation means something more than merely the impact of physical stimulus (for example, light) on receptors (eyeballs), it must be carried out within an organizing framework of fundamentals. As Chalmers puts it:

> Observation statements must be made in the language of some theory, however vague. Consider the simple sentence in commonsense language, 'Look out, the

wind is blowing the baby's pram over the cliff edge!' Much low-level theory is presupposed here. It is implied that there is such a thing as wind, which has the property of being able to cause the motion of objects such as prams, which stand in its path. The sense of urgency conveyed by the 'look out' indicates the expectation that the pram, complete with baby, will fall over the cliff and perhaps be dashed on the rocks and it is further assumed that this will be deleterious for the baby. (1982: 28–9)

Financial statements are not immune from the theory dependence of observation. The idea that, behind the specific numbers included in individual financial reports, there are relatively abstract generalizations about the accounting world, is not novel. For example, in setting out four 'fundamental accounting concepts', defined as 'broad basic assumptions which underlie the periodic financial accounts of business enterprises', SSAP2 was careful to emphasize that these were not new principles to be added to the set of regulations already in existence, but rather were already 'regarded as having general acceptability' (paragraph 14).

This book takes the view that, since some, more or less systematic, structure of abstract propositions about the accounting world is an inevitable component of financial reporting practice, it is helpful if this structure (accounting theory) is made explicit and tested for rigour and consistency. Accordingly, our purpose is to examine the structure of modern financial reporting theory, and subject it to critical scrutiny.

But how are we to discover what this theory is? It is not necessarily an easy task to identify the systems of reasoning actually used by individual accountants as they go about their tasks. However, we do know a good deal about the system that the UK body responsible for setting financial reporting standards (the Accounting Standards Board) 'believes should underlie the preparation and presentation of . . . financial statements' (SP, Introduction, paragraph 1) and will use in its 'development and review of accounting standards' (SP, Introduction, paragraph 2). We know about this particular theory because the Board itself has provided an explicit statement of it in the form of a Statement of Principles, published in December 1999. Clearly, the theory adopted by the Board will play a major role in shaping financial reporting practice in the UK. Hence it is the Board's theory that is the major subject of this book.

Theories that have been set down by standard-setting agencies are sometimes referred to informally as 'conceptual frameworks' and we will be using that term (among others) to describe the Statement of Principles issued by the Accounting Standards Board (ASB). Other standard-setting bodies around the world have also adopted conceptual frameworks but we will not be paying very much attention to these, or to rival theories proposed as alternatives to the Board's position, except to the extent that they help in elucidating the Board's framework. We will look at the way the Board's conceptual framework fits with existing practice and with other 'principles' espoused by the profession. We shall not be addressing the wider task of constructing what were referred to earlier in this section as theories of accounting.

The rediscovery of usefulness

The early development of financial accounting was essentially a pragmatic process, geared to assisting proprietors, who were then the main users of accounts, to keep track of their resources. The preparation of financial statements was carried out principally as a check on the accuracy of the bookkeeping, rather than to measure performance and position (see, for example, Edwards, 1989: Chapters 5 and 6).

The emergence of large-scale enterprises in the nineteenth century, and the consequent separation of ownership and management control, created a need for financial statements for the purpose of accountability, that is to ensure that managers rendered a reliable account of their activities to owners. Prior to this period, if a measure of performance was needed, it was not uncommon for it to be arrived at by valuing assets and liabilities directly, computing the net asset position at two different dates, and comparing one with the other to arrive at profit. The constraints under which the emerging process of accounting for large-scale enterprises operated, however, discouraged this approach. It was felt that 'objective' figures were needed (in contrast to subjective valuations); there was a need to limit the scope for management manipulation and to promote the 'auditability' of the figures; and the use of accounting information to justify dividend payments linked profitability to liquidity and a concern with the realization of gains. For these reasons, the emerging system focused principally on tracking the cost of resources obtained and used by the business and on matching cost with the revenues realized by the business through time – the 'historical cost-realized revenue' approach (see, Edwards, 1989: Chapter 10). Under this system a variety of specialist accounting procedures are employed to measure and allocate costs against revenue.

By the middle of the twentieth century, financial accounting had moved a long way from its utilitarian origins: accountants had come to focus more on the internal technical structure of the system, so that the design of accounting procedures had become an end in itself. One leading academic critic of financial reporting was able to ridicule the British profession by providing a montage of official pronouncements apparently taking pride in the uselessness of financial reports:

A balance sheet does not purport to show the realisable value of assets . . . A balance sheet is not a statement of the net worth of the undertaking . . . The results are not a measure of the increase or decrease in wealth in terms of purchasing power; nor do the results necessarily represent the amount which can prudently be regarded as available for distribution . . . Similarly the results shown by . . . accounts are not necessarily suitable for purposes such as price-fixing, wage negotiations and taxation . . . The purpose for which annual accounts are normally prepared is not to enable individual shareholders to take investment decisions. (adapted from Stamp, 1970: 101–2)

Viewed now from the perspective of the new century, it is difficult to appreciate just how far practice had moved from any real concern with usefulness.

The revival of interest in the pursuit of usefulness can be traced to the publication in 1966 of a report by the American Accounting Association, a body consisting mainly of academics. This set out a, now famous, definition of accounting as:

the process of identifying, measuring and communicating economic information to permit informed judgements and decisions by users of the information. (1966: 1)

Writing at the time of publication of the report, Robert Sterling, a distinguished financial accounting theorist, observed that 'this is a change in "world view" and is the stuff that revolutions are made of' (1967: 100).

One report does not make a revolution in accountancy, especially when it comes from academia. Within a decade, however, professional bodies were beginning to address questions of usefulness, although, at least at first, the reports covering this ground emerged from working parties and discussion groups that had no claim to speak authoritatively for the profession as a whole. Probably the first group established by a professional body to issue a report on the objectives of financial reporting, expressed in terms of the provision of useful information, was the Study Group on the Objectives of Financial Statements (the Trueblood Committee) of the American Institute of Certified Public Accountants, which published its findings in 1973.

Two years later, a discussion paper issued by the UK Accounting Standards Steering Committee (a forerunner of the ASB) *began* with the words:

Our basic approach has been that corporate reports should seek to satisfy, as far as possible, the information needs of users: they should be useful. (1975: 15)

The idea that financial statements should be useful had reached British shores. This idea now underpins the ASB's conceptual framework and thus its efforts to reform British accounting practice.

The emergence of conceptual frameworks

Academics, standard-setting agencies and others have been offering statements about the principles that do – or should – underpin financial reporting for many years, and in many countries. However, the first such statement to qualify as an agreed conceptual framework in the sense used in this chapter was the US Financial Accounting Standards Board's set of Statements of Financial Accounting Concepts. This was developed over a period of a decade, commencing in the mid 1970s.[1] It took, as its starting point, the work of the Trueblood Committee, referred to earlier. Development of the framework represented a very substantial project for the FASB. Some idea of the scale of the work can be obtained from the funding devoted to it: at its peak, the project was absorbing some 40% of the total budget of the organization, which itself amounted to about $8 million per annum. In other words, at 2000 price levels, expenditure was in the order of several million pounds a year (Macve, 1981: 95).

Subsequent to the pioneering work of the FASB, many standard-setting bodies in countries employing Anglo-American style financial reporting have issued agreed conceptual frameworks, albeit under a variety of names. Countries which now have agreed conceptual frameworks include Australia (early 1990s), Canada (1988) and New Zealand (mid 1990s). In addition, the International Accounting Standards Committee (IASC) adopted its own framework in 1989. Though there are differences between them, all the frameworks listed in this section are broadly consistent with each other and with the ASB's Statement of Principles.

The consistency between the different frameworks developed internationally provides some comfort that the British document is working along the right lines. It will also promote the international harmonization of accounting standards, since the various national bodies will be working within essentially the same framework. This is of particular relevance to the work of the so-called G4+1, an international group consisting of the standard-setting bodies of Australia, Canada, New Zealand, the UK and the USA, with the IASC as observers (the title refers to the fact that, on its foundation, there were four national bodies with the IASC as observer being the 'plus one'). This group is seeking to adopt common solutions to financial reporting problems, and in particular to align financial reporting standards across its members' jurisdictions. In pursuit of this objective, membership of the group requires that bodies adopt a conceptual framework similar to those of the other members (see the G4+1 Memorandum of Understanding on Objectives included, for example, in the ASB DP, *Business Combinations*). We shall be looking at some of the issues considered by G4+1 in subsequent chapters.

The role of a conceptual framework

It is possible to identify a number of roles or purposes for accounting theories in general, and for conceptual frameworks in particular. If a theory or framework could be stated in terms that were sufficiently rigorous and comprehensive, it could determine the structure and content of actual financial statements. It could thus sweep aside the corpus of legislative requirements, accounting standards and other authoritative pronouncements, established procedures and subsidiary semi-authoritative guidelines that currently determine the structure and content of financial statements and that we know as *generally accepted accounting practice* (GAAP). In practice, none of the theories and frameworks developed by standard-setters, academics or others have achieved this condition. Indeed, as we shall see in later chapters, there are good reasons for assuming that a theory of this nature, whether or not it would be a good thing to have in principle, will remain elusive for a long time to come.

In the absence of a theory that leads directly to the accounting numbers to be inserted in concrete financial statements, standard-setters have sought frameworks whose primary role is to support the development of accounting standards. Under this approach, the framework is used to shape accounting standards and the standards are then applied in preparing individual financial statements. This is the approach adopted by the ASB in the UK. It follows that the framework, whatever its title, is not itself an accounting standard and is not part of the mandatory requirements accountants must follow in preparing financial statements. Indeed, *as far as this primary function is concerned*, accountants need not be familiar with, or even have heard of, the framework:[2] they will be applying its principles by following the standards derived from it.

Clearly, a conceptual framework is not an essential prerequisite to setting accounting standards: standard-setters in the UK have been producing standards for several decades without one. Why, then have standard-setters around the world sought to adopt conceptual frameworks? The principal way in which the framework should aid standard-setting is in helping standard-setters to get it *right*: to adopt the particular method, approach, disclosure requirements, and so on that best assist users of statements. As the US framework puts it:

> The conceptual framework . . . is expected to serve the public interest by providing structure and direction to financial accounting and reporting to facilitate the provision of even-handed financial and related information that helps promote the efficient allocation of scarce resources in the economy and society, including assisting capital and other markets to function efficiently. (SFAC6, Preface, paragraph 2)

Although the British Statement of Principles does not contain such a bold and explicit affirmation of its underlying purpose, the American approach quoted here applies equally well to the British project.

Within the broad purpose identified in the previous paragraph, we can identify a number of contributions a conceptual framework can make to standard-setting:

1   Because standards are developed within the framework, they should be more consistent with each other and represent a more coherent overall approach to the problems of financial reporting (SP, Introduction, paragraph 1).
2   By establishing agreement on fundamental issues, the framework should avoid the need to debate these issues every time a standard is under development (SP, Introduction, paragraph 3).
3   The framework communicates to other parties to the standard-setting process (for example, preparers who may wish to make submissions on an exposure draft) the standard-setters' thinking on fundamental issues and may thus help them to see why a standard or exposure draft takes a particular line (SP, Introduction, paragraph 4).

As well as the primary purpose of aiding standard-setters, conceptual frameworks can fulfil several secondary purposes:

1   They provide an authoritative statement of the fundamental concepts that underlie financial reporting. For example, as we shall see later, the British Statement incorporates definitions of such primitive accounting terms as *assets* and *liabilities*, and this is the first time that authoritative definitions of these terms have been established in the UK (see Chapter 4).[3] It does seem surprising that an authoritative definition of the term 'asset' has not previously been available to accountants trying to decide whether individual items do or do not constitute assets. The availability of such an authoritative statement can add to the public's confidence in financial reporting generally and in the corpus of accounting standards.
2   They help to communicate standard-setters' overall aims and views, as well as the concepts which underpin accounting standards.
3   They help accountants (and, of key importance for most readers of this volume, students of accountancy) to understand why and how financial reporting operates in the way that it does – at least when it operates as the standard-setters envisage that it should.
4   They provide a commonly understood (and, it is to be hoped, widely accepted) working vocabulary with which to discuss issues within financial reporting, such as those raised by specific exposure drafts.
5   While not, in themselves, part of the system of mandatory rules, they can assist preparers, auditors and others to judge how emerging issues and problems, not yet the subject of standards, should be dealt with (SP, Introduction, paragraph 4).

The nature of conceptual frameworks

We can again turn to the USA for an explanation of the nature of the type of conceptual framework adopted there and in the UK. The explanation applies equally well to the British framework, whose own discussion is rather briefer:

> The conceptual framework is a coherent system of interrelated objectives and fundamentals that . . . prescribes the nature, function and limits of financial accounting and reporting . . . The objectives identify the goals and purposes of financial reporting. The fundamentals are the underlying concepts of financial accounting – concepts that guide the selection of transactions, events and circumstances to be accounted for; their recognition and measurement; and the means of summarising and communicating them to interested parties. Concepts of this type are fundamental in the sense that other concepts flow from them and repeated reference to them will be necessary in establishing, interpreting and applying accounting and reporting standards. (SFAC6, Preface, paragraphs 1–2, material reordered)

It is worth reflecting at this point on what the ASB's conceptual framework, like all the other conceptual frameworks for financial reporting developed by standard-setters, is *not*. It is a theory in the sense that it is an abstract system of reasoning; it is not a theory in the sense of being a statement of empirical regularities with predictive power, like the theories of natural science. We use the theory for the purposes described in the previous section. We do not use it to make predictions, as natural scientists do when they predict how two chemicals mixed together will react. Equally, we do not test it by determining if its predictions correspond to what actually occurs under specified conditions.

This is not to say that an accounting theory, or a conceptual framework, would be very satisfactory if it had no correspondence with our perceptions of the world in which we were expecting to use it and no predictive power of any kind. Because it is underpinned by the notion of usefulness, we would expect the theory to draw on claims about why, when and how financial statements are used that have some correspondence with what we believe actually goes on. We would also expect the theory to make claims about the consequences of applying its logic that could, in principle at least, be empirically tested. In practice, the empirical testing of usefulness has proved extremely challenging but, at a minimum, we would expect the theory to make *some* claims about the world in which financial statements are prepared and used and for those claims to be plausible to those familiar with this world. The extent to which this expectation is met is discussed as the theory is set out in later chapters of this book.

We would also expect the theory to have some power to predict how accounting standards will evolve, given that standard-setters claim that they will be guided by it: in that sense too, the theory should have some empirical grounding and if, after a number of years, it is shown to have no capacity whatsoever to predict the content of accounting standards, we may come to doubt the standard-setters' insistence that they are seeking to apply it.

The status and scope of the Statement of Principles

A number of points about the status and scope of the ASB's Statement of Principles need to be borne in mind in appreciating its arguments. The first, which we have already alluded to, is that it is not intended to be a mandatory pronouncement to be followed in preparing actual financial statements. As a consequence, in analysing its content we need to ask not how that content is to be applied in drawing up statements but rather how it is to be applied in developing standards.

The Statement applies to profit-oriented entities, including public sector bodies with such an orientation, regardless of size. It covers *general purpose* financial statements: this term is intended to exclude from the scope of the framework statements drawn up under requirements specified by the recipient, such as tax returns and filings to regulatory agencies. Although the contents of the Statement of Principles will have some relevance to financial reports beyond the strict financial statements (such as chief executives' commentaries) and to not-for-profit entities, for our purposes we can think of the primary scope of the Statement as being the full annual financial statements of limited companies. It also applies to other financial statements intended to be consistent with the annual statements, such as interim reports, but in such cases further considerations may also be relevant: for example, in the case of interim reports, specific problems can arise from the need to account for a period shorter than the financial year.

The Statement of Principles and current GAAP

The Statement of Principles is broadly consistent with current GAAP in the sense that, if current GAAP were amended to embody the minimum of changes necessary to align it with the Statement, financial statements drawn up in accordance with the revised GAAP would, in the main, resemble those drawn up under current GAAP. There would be a profit and loss account, a balance sheet and a cash flow statement; these statements would contain income and expense, assets and liabilities, and so on; individual items would be measured more or less as now.

A cynical view might be that the Statement has been designed with this end in mind. Certainly a Statement which challenged most or all of the fundamental tenets of financial reporting as currently undertaken would struggle to gain acceptance by the profession. As we examine the key features of the Statement, we will ask whether it is surprising, from a functional point of view, that its prescriptions should resemble current practice – and, for the most part, we will see that a plausible case can be made that the broad features of contemporary practice are appropriate to the tasks of financial reporting.

However, not all the detail of the Statement is consistent with GAAP: there are inconsistencies with current accounting standards and practices, with some of the concepts underpinning them, and with legal requirements. The ASB quite deliberately adopted the approach of working from principles to prescription, rather than 'reverse engineering' its principles to be compatible with current requirements and practices. Standards and the law can change, and the objective is that the Statement can influence those changes for the better. This objective could not be achieved if it was simply designed to embody the current position (SP, Appendix I, paragraph 3).

At the same time, the law is a major constraint on financial reporting and a conceptual framework which had major inconsistencies with current law would be of limited value in developing accounting standards. Fortunately, this problem does not arise with the Statement of Principles.

We will examine the main differences between the Statement of Principles and the concepts and fundamentals underpinning current GAAP as we look at each component of the framework in turn.

The Statement of Principles and the standard-setting process

As we have seen, the main purpose of the Statement of Principles is to assist in the standard-setting process, but the ASB is careful to point out that new standards will not necessarily follow the Statement of Principles exactly. The Statement lists a number of other issues that arise in practice in setting a standard. Perhaps the most important of these is the cost–benefit criterion. Financial reporting rules generally impose costs (for example the cost of preparing the information) and ought to yield benefits (principally the better quality of decisions taken as a result of having better information). A strict application of all the principles in the Statement at all times could push the costs of preparing information beyond the point at which costs and benefits are appropriately balanced (we will return to this point in Chapter 3).

Other constraints on the application of the Statement of Principles listed by the ASB (SP, Introduction, paragraph 14) include current legal requirements (see the previous section), any issues that may arise in respect of specific industries, and difficulties in implementing the methods that the Statement would suggest are desirable. A further consideration is the Board's commitment, as set out in its Statement of Aims, to 'take account of the desire of the financial community for evolutionary rather than revolutionary change in the reporting process' (ASB SOA, Fundamental Guidelines, paragraph 7), in so far as this is consistent with its objectives. This means that changes needed to fully reflect the contents of the Statement of Principles might need to be introduced gradually.

Alternative views of the conceptual framework project

A number of commentators have challenged the motivation and purpose of the conceptual framework projects undertaken in the USA and elsewhere. The principal criticism has been that frameworks are in fact merely a political device, intended to give legitimacy and credibility to the standard-setting bodies and their standards or to stave off government intervention in the allegedly cosy world of financial reporting (see, for example, Dopuch and Sunder, 1980). An alternative way of putting essentially the same argument is that frameworks are a rhetorical tool, designed to support standard-setters' claims to knowledge rather than actually to embody knowledge independently arrived at. For these commentators, individual financial reporting standards are irremediably the outcome of a power struggle between interest groups; conceptual frameworks mask rather than supplant this process.

It is difficult to deny that there is a political dimension to the standard-setting process. However, as Power (1993) points out, the force of criticisms of conceptual framework projects made by commentators such as Dopuch and Sunder is achieved by imposing very demanding tests on those frameworks: essentially it is asserted that it should be possible to settle all accounting policy issues by resorting only to the logic of the framework, and if the framework fails this test it is argued that there must have been some other motivation – presumably political – for its adoption. This is a very stringent test indeed and may well be one that no conceivable conceptual framework could pass.

An intermediate position would be that the conceptual frameworks of the UK and elsewhere are best seen, not as mechanisms for resolving, by themselves, all accounting policy issues, but rather as one important element in a set of arrangements – some of which may, inevitably, be political – that, taken together, have the capacity to improve the quality of accounting standards (see, for example, Gaa, 1988). This position is sufficient to justify supporting and seeking to understand the ASB's Statement of Principles and is the view taken in this book.

Notes

1 An exposure draft of a new Statement covering the use of discounting in financial statements was issued in 1997.

2 Before readers snap this book shut with relief, it should be pointed out that a number of the secondary purposes of the framework require that accountants should be familiar with its content.

3 The Accounting Standards Committee agreed to recognize the IASC's conceptual framework (which contains definitions of terms such as assets) as 'a set of guidelines to assist it in its work of developing proposals for new standards and revisions to existing standards' (ASC Foreword to the IASC Framework for the Preparation and Presentation of Financial Statements, paragraph 3), but this

commitment was not carried over to its successor, the Accounting Standards Board. In any event the degree of recognition implicit in the ASC's position was somewhat limited.

References

Accounting Standards Steering Committee (1975) *The Corporate Report*. London: Accounting Standards Steering Committee.

American Accounting Association (1966) *A Statement of Basic Accounting Theory*. Sarasota, FL: American Accounting Association.

American Institute of Certified Public Accountants (1973) *Report of the Study Group on the Objectives of Financial Statements*. New York: American Institute of Certified Public Accountants.

Chalmers, A.F. (1982) *What Is This Thing Called Science?*, 2nd edn. Milton Keynes: Open University Press.

Dopuch, N. and Sunder, S. (1980) 'FASB's Statement on Objectives and Elements of Financial Accounting: a review', *Accounting Review*, 1–21.

Edwards, J.R. (1989) *A History of Financial Accounting*. London: Routledge.

Gaa, J.C. (1988) *Methodological Foundations of Standard-Setting for Corporate Financial Reporting*. Sarasota, FL: American Accounting Association.

Macve, R. (1981) *A Conceptual Framework of Financial Accounting and Reporting*. London: Institute of Chartered Accountants in England and Wales.

Most, K.S. (1982) *Accounting Theory*, 2nd edn. Columbus, OH: Grid.

Power, M.K. (1993) 'The idea of a conceptual framework', in M.J. Mumford and K.V. Peasnell (eds), *Philosophical Perspectives on Accounting: Essays in Honour of Edward Stamp*. London: Routledge.

Stamp, E. (1970) 'Establishing accounting principles', *Abacus*, 96–104.

Sterling, R.R. (1967) '"A Statement of Basic Accounting Theory": a review article', *Journal of Accounting Research*, 95–112.

Further reading

For a brief survey of some other countries' conceptual frameworks, see M. Davies, R. Paterson and A. Wilson, *UK GAAP*, 6th edn, London: Macmillan, 1999.

A number of useful surveys of theories of accounting are available. One which focuses on economic models is W.H. Beaver, *Financial Reporting: an Accounting Revolution*, 3rd edn, Upper Saddle River, NJ: Prentice-Hall, 1998. For a more wide-ranging survey, see A.R. Belkaoui, *Accounting Theory*, 4th edn, London: Thomson Learning, 2000.

For an interesting (but challenging) discussion of some of the philosophical issues that arise in considering conceptual frameworks, see the chapters by M.K. Power and S. Archer in M.J. Mumford and K.V. Peasnell (eds), *Philosophical Perspectives on Accounting: Essays in Honour of Edward Stamp*, London: Routledge, 1993.

2

The Objective of Financial Statements

We saw in Chapter 1 that the development of conceptual frameworks by accounting standard-setters has been driven by the notion that the financial reporting process should be useful. In the ASB's words:

> Put simply, the objective of financial statements is to provide information that is useful to those for whom they are prepared. (SP, p. 16)

Important though this general principle is, it does not take us very far, in itself, towards specifying the content of financial statements. In order to do this, we need to answer two key questions:

1   Who are the users of financial statements?
2   What uses do they make of financial statements?

This chapter addresses these questions.

Users of financial statements

Many different groups have direct or indirect relationships with a modern business corporation. These include suppliers of capital (both equity and loan capital); suppliers of other resources; employees; customers; and government agencies. The public generally may also be affected by a corporation's affairs. For example, members of the public may be adversely affected by pollution generated by the corporation or may benefit indirectly from the employment it creates, perhaps by obtaining work in the local services sector as a result of extra demand created by expansion in the corporation's activities. As well as those parties currently engaged in relationships with the corporation, others may have a potential relationship, for example because they are considering making an investment. Further, some groups have an indirect relationship because they act as advisers, or provide information, to those who have a direct relationship: for example financial analysts advise actual and potential investors and newspapers provide information to investors and other parties.

Anyone who has a relationship with a particular entity can be affected by what happens to it and hence may find information about its affairs useful. Some of the parties listed earlier may be able to insist on receiving information specially tailored to suit their needs: for example, bankers may demand specific information as a condition for making a loan. This sort of information is contained in 'special purpose financial reports' and, as we saw in Chapter 1, such reports fall outside the scope of the Statement of Principles. Most parties, however, are not in a position to impose such a condition on their relationship with the entity and, if they need financial information, they must rely on the general purpose financial reports (including the general purpose financial statements) produced by the entity for general circulation.

In the case of equity investors (shareholders) and those considering making an equity investment (potential investors), it is easy to see that financial information is likely to be useful. We will examine the way in which information might be used shortly, but it seems probable that investors and potential investors, whose motivation for investment is the financial return they will receive from their investment, would wish both (a) to evaluate the past financial performance of the corporation (for example, to determine whether its management has operated effectively); and (b) to arrive at a view about likely future performance.

It is not perhaps quite so obvious why other parties would want financial information about an entity. Even lenders might be thought to have little interest in a company's performance: after all they are legally entitled to have their interest paid as it falls due and they will also generally be entitled to the return of principal in accordance with their loan agreement or be able to sell their investment on to a third party, backed up by legal rights to further interest payments. Why would they be concerned about the overall performance of the company? The reason is, of course, that a legal right to interest and the return of principal will be of little value if the company's overall performance is so poor that it does not have the cash to make the necessary payments to its lenders: hence lenders will want to evaluate, on the basis of past performance and future prospects, what the risk of this occurring might be.

It is possible to identify, in principle, ways in which the other parties identified earlier in this section might use information about the company's financial performance. Like lenders, suppliers who provide goods and services on credit will be concerned with the risk that they might not be paid. Suppliers (whether or not they grant credit) and customers may be interested in evaluating whether a company is likely to continue to purchase from them, or supply to them, for example if they need to set up specialist equipment to supply the goods, or to manufacture goods from the materials being supplied, so that there is a risk of some loss if the company terminates its relationship with them. Equally, employees may be interested in knowing how secure their employment is, and what level of remuneration to seek, and these will depend, in part, on the future of the company.

A conceptual framework for financial reporting built on usefulness can seek to incorporate the needs of a wide range of potential users, such as that discussed above, or focus on a narrower and more specific range. This is a point in the construction of the framework at which its architects have a choice: even if some group can be shown to use financial statements, it does not follow that their interests necessarily have to be taken into account. If a wide range of users is embraced, there is a potential difficulty if their needs turn out to be diverse (making the specification of the framework complex) or if it is difficult to identify the needs of some of the groups (so that the framework becomes impossible to complete).

On the other hand, focusing on a narrow range of users makes for a relatively simple and rigorously specified framework. Where it can be demonstrated that the potential users actually do use financial statements, and the purpose for which the statements are used is well documented, the construction of the conceptual framework is made a good deal easier. However, such a focus might be thought to be unfair and exclusive and thereby reduce support for the framework and the work of the standard-setting body.

The ASB attempts to escape from this dilemma in the following way. The obvious candidate for a 'narrow-range' user group is equity investors. Company law requires that the annual financial statements of companies are distributed to current shareholders and no other group is identified in this way. It is often suggested that the position of shareholders means that the accounts are prepared for them – though since the legislation also requires that a copy be put on the public record (by filing at Companies House), it is clear that the law envisages that they will be made more generally available, presumably for other users. As we shall see, there is a considerable body of empirical evidence that investors and potential investors do use financial statements and some evidence as to how they are used.

The Statement of Principles identifies investors as the *defining class* of user. It means by this that, in constructing the conceptual framework, the use made of financial statements by investors will generally be taken as establishing what information is needed. The Statement asserts that 'the perspective from which investors view financial performance and financial position . . . is also of fundamental importance to other users' (SP, 1.10). From this it follows that financial statements that

> focus on the interest that investors have in the reporting entity's financial performance and financial position will, in effect, also be focusing on the common interest that all users have in that entity's financial performance and financial position. (SP, 1.11)

In other words, by satisfying the information needs of investors, financial statements can also satisfy needs of other users. The Statement says that it is adopting a 'rebuttable assumption' (SP, 1.11) that this is the case: in other words, should the logic not hold in any particular situation, an alternative approach would be adopted. However, there is no point in the rest of the framework at which an alternative view of information needs is in fact taken, implying that the ASB considers that the assumption holds for all the content of financial statements. Whether this, rather strong, contention is appropriate will be examined later in this chapter.

The objective of financial statements

Investors and potential investors are likely to be interested in obtaining information about an entity in order to assist them in deciding whether to increase or reduce their investment in that entity: they need information to take an economic decision. They may also wish to assess the stewardship of management, for example, to determine whether management has made effective use of the resources entrusted to it. This assessment may cover a variety of factors including both the safeguarding and proper use of resources and their efficient and effective use to maximize profitability. The assessment will, however, in turn feed into an economic decision. This decision may be of a different kind to the investment decision, for example it may be the decision to replace management if it is under-performing. Alternatively, the assessment may simply feed through into the investment decision: if management's stewardship is good this may contribute to a decision to invest further; if it is poor, investors may decide to sell their shares. The nature of the economic decisions to be taken by investors suggests that the sort of information needed will include information about the financial performance and financial position of the entity.

We have examined a range of purposes for which other groups with an interest in the entity might need information about that entity and these purposes can also be characterized as taking economic decisions. For example, lenders need to decide whether or not to lend to the entity or to increase or decrease their lending, together with the terms on which they will lend; suppliers need to decide whether to build new or adapt existing capacity to cater for the particular requirements of a customer; and employees need to decide whether to seek work elsewhere or to press for a pay rise. Again, the nature of the decisions to be taken suggests that the sort of information needed will include information about the financial performance and position of the entity.

The Statement of Principles accepts that 'different decisions usually require different information' (SP, 1.5) but, as we have seen, it then argues that there is sufficient overlap between the information requirements of different groups to mean that there is a 'common interest' in the sort of information required by investors. As a result, it is able to summarize the position as follows:

> The objective of financial statements is to provide information about the reporting entity's financial performance and financial position that is useful to a wide range of users for assessing the stewardship of the entity's management and for making economic decisions. (SP, p. 16)

Given the Statement's focus on economic decision-making, it is curious that it should place the assessment of stewardship before decision-making in formally setting out the objective of financial statements. This ordering may reflect the outcome of a political battle between those who prefer the vaguer formulation of 'assessing stewardship' to the more clear-cut and thus potentially demanding approach based on identifying economic decisions and the information inputs required to take them. Auditors might, for example, fear that adoption of the decision-usefulness approach could lead to litigation from users who consider that information they received caused them to take an incorrect investment decision.

Investors' information needs

At one level, the information needs of investors can be specified very simply. Investors buy shares in a company to make gains. They receive these gains in two ways: (a) by receiving dividends from the company itself; and (b) from increases in the value of their shares. They receive the gain from dividends directly from the company itself and, if the company is quoted on a stock exchange, they can observe the size of the change in value of their shares by monitoring prices on the exchange. Ultimately, though, whether the company is quoted or not, the only way in which they receive gains from changing value is by selling shares to a third party. Thus the company-specific information needed by someone considering buying shares in a company is (a) the price of the shares now; (b) the price of the shares at some point in the future (let us call this point t_1); and (c) the level of dividend paid between now and t_1. If the gain reflected by the dividends to be received and the change in price between now and t_1 exceeds the gains available from other investments, a rational investor will buy the shares; otherwise, not. If the time horizon is very short (say between today and tomorrow), so that the time value of money can be ignored and no dividends become payable, and if transaction costs are immaterial and the investor has sufficient cash available, the 'decision rule' becomes very simple: if tomorrow's price exceeds today's, buy; if today's price exceeds tomorrow's, do not buy, and if some shares are already held, sell them.

As events unfold, investors will receive the information specified in the previous paragraph without needing to consult the company's financial statements. Investors will have the necessary information about dividends because they will actually receive the cash; they will have the information about prices either from actual transactions (buying and selling their shares) or from monitoring stock exchange reports. Although financial statements, as currently prepared, do contain information about dividends, investors will not need to consult them for this purpose, and such statements do not even contain information about the company's share price movements. On the face of it, then, this model of investors' information needs suggests that financial statements are unnecessary because the desired information can be obtained elsewhere.

However there is a major snag: in order to be useful, investors need the information *before* events unfold. The future is, of course, uncertain, so that they simply cannot be given the information that the decision model specifies. Instead, the best that can be done is to feed *predictions* of the specified parameters into the decision model. One way of doing this would be for the company's managers to publish predictions. There are several difficulties about such an approach. Managers' predictions may be biased; for example they may be tempted to understate the extent of any difficulties they foresee, and the consequent reduction in dividends and share price, to postpone the point at which investors might try to have them replaced. Managers might be reluctant to publish forecasts for fear that, however honest they are in preparing them, angry investors will sue if they turn out to be wrong; alternatively, for fear of being sued if forecasts turn out to be too high, managers might consistently understate likely gains. Though this caution might be justified under the circumstances, it nonetheless represents bias and would result in erroneous outcomes from the decision rule. Individual investors are essentially trying to achieve gains by making better investment decisions than other investors, yet if everybody uses the same predictions (as published by managers), the decision rule will yield the same result for everybody and the share price will either soar (as everybody tries to buy) or plummet (as everybody tries to sell). What individual investors really want to do is get to the right decision just ahead of everybody else.

For all these reasons, in practice companies typically do not publish forecasts of the information needed: rather investors and potential investors use forecasts prepared either by themselves or by specialists employed for the purpose. These are *financial analysts*, who may work for the investor (usually only when a large institutional investor such as a pension fund or insurance company is involved), for a third party, perhaps a financial institution providing advice as part of a package designed to encourage the investor to use its services, or for the financial press.

Investors and financial analysts are, then, essentially interested in forecasting future dividends over some period and share price movements between the beginning and end of that period. Share prices themselves reflect the market's expectations of the returns to be received from the shares, that is, dividends. Thus in forecasting the price of shares at the end of the period, we are essentially forecasting what the market believes the shares will pay in dividends from that point onwards. In other words, forecasting dividends *and* share price movements can be reduced to forecasting dividend streams over a long time horizon. It is possible to forecast dividends and share price movements statistically from past values without resorting to financial statements. Remember, though, that each investor is trying to make a better forecast than the others – and because, directly or indirectly, analysts are selling their services to investors, they are also trying to make better forecasts than their competitors.

In general terms, future dividends and share price movements are likely to be closely related to the future financial performance of the company, expressed in terms of its ability to obtain more resources from selling its output than it consumes in producing it. Future dividends will be paid from future surpluses and the larger the future surpluses, the larger the dividends can be. Payment of dividends will require cash and the capacity of the company to generate cash will heavily influence its ability to pay dividends. Increases in share price will reflect the market's increased estimation of the company's ability to provide future income for investors – in other words, future dividends. This ability comes from increases in the company's resource base, which can come from past surpluses, or, put another way, from net cash inflows, not paid out in dividends. Thus the generation of surpluses and associated net cash inflows can drive increases in dividends and increases in share price. It seems plausible then, and is widely accepted, that information about the company's ability to generate financial surpluses and associated net cash inflows can contribute to increasing the quality of forecasts of the company's dividends and share price movements.

It is not suggested that the company's past financial performance is the *only* determinant of changes in share price: for example, changes in the economic climate generally may affect share prices and different companies may be affected by a change in economic climate in different ways (and thus experience different changes in share price). This simply means that investors may need other sources of information in addition to that concerning the financial performance of the company.

If an investor knew tomorrow's share price, there seems little reason to doubt that he or she would use this information directly in the decision rule outlined earlier. Since this is not known, a variety of possible combinations of information type and decision rules may be employed. The investor may focus on any of the following, each of which will be, as we have seen, substitutable for the others to a greater or lesser extent:

1   dividends and share price movement over a period
2   the dividend stream over a long time horizon

3   company earnings, representing the company's ability to pay dividends or reinvest
4   company cash flows, representing the company's capacity to fund dividends or reinvestment.

It is important to remember that, although the ultimate basis for returns to the investor is the company's ability to generate cash, cash generating ability and financial performance expressed in terms of earnings are closely related.

Arnold and Moizer's survey of UK financial analysts between 1978 and 1981 found that:

> the [method] adopted by most analysts involves an attempt to identify shares which seem to be over- or under-valued. In order to calculate a value [that is, share price] with which to compare the current market value [that is, share price], a company's earnings for a subsequent year calculated on a historical cost basis are first estimated. A PE [price/earnings] ratio, apparently based heavily on the analyst's experience and judgement, is then applied to estimated earnings to obtain an estimate of future market value. (1984: 205)

The PE ratio can be calculated on the basis of the current share price and latest published earnings: for example a company with earnings (essentially profit after interest, taxation and preference dividends) of £10 million, 20 million shares and a share price of £2, would have earnings per share of 50p (£10 million divided by 20 million shares) and a PE ratio of 4 (£2/0.50). If, as explained above, earnings find their way to investors in the form either of dividends or of increases in share price, the PE ratio reflects the number of years before an outlay on purchasing shares is recouped or, put another way, the number of years' future earnings being purchased. The ratio thus reflects 'market sentiment' about the company: the riskier the investment, the lower will be the PE ratio because buyers will want to recoup their investment earlier in the face of risk; equally, the better the growth prospects, the higher will be the PE ratio because investors will actually get their returns sooner than is implicit in a ratio based on current earnings.

Continuing the very simple example given above, if an analyst is confident that the PE ratio of 4 is appropriate for the company, given the level of risk involved and other factors, and forecasts next year's earnings at £12 million or 60p per share, her or his forecast of next year's share price will be £0.60 × 4 = £2.40.[1] The analyst's recommendation will therefore be to buy shares now at £2.00 to yield a gain of 40p over the year (ignoring transaction costs, the time value of money, and other investment opportunities). Put the other way round, the growth prospects in earnings mean that the analyst would be prepared to see a higher PE ratio on current earnings: once the price has risen to £2.40, the

PE ratio on current earnings will be £2.40/0.50 = 4.8. Thus, as explained in the previous paragraph, growth prospects support a higher PE ratio.

Notice that this particular model involves predicting amounts actually found in the financial statements, namely earnings. It differs somewhat from the model described earlier, which involved forecasting future dividends and (possibly) share price movements. However, as we have seen, since future dividends are linked to financial performance, the two models may be compatible, provided that the PE ratio appropriately reflects the expected pattern of future growth in dividends and factors such as the time value of money and risk.

Whether investors and analysts forecast future dividends and (possibly) share price movements directly, or employ some other method such as the 'earnings and PE ratio' model described in the previous paragraphs, the Statement of Principles argues that they will be able to make better quality forecasts if they use information about a company's financial performance, financial position, generation and use of cash and financial adaptability. We will consider each of these factors in turn.

Financial performance

The Statement of Principles defines *financial performance* as follows:

> The financial performance of an entity comprises the return it obtains on the resources it controls, the components of that return and the characteristics of those components. (SP, 1.13)

This definition does not employ established accounting terminology, and thus avoids begging the question as to whether what is already reported in financial statements is appropriate. However, by way of illustrating the sorts of information involved here, we might think of 'the return' as comprising total gains and losses, 'the components' as being operating profit, financial income, extraordinary items, and so on, and 'the characteristics' as including factors such as stability from one period to another. It is emphasized that this is not to argue that the terms in this definition can be read directly across to conventional financial statements, but merely to illustrate the sorts of ideas under discussion.

We have seen that investors are ultimately interested in future returns to themselves, rather than past returns to the company. Why, then, might they be interested in information about the latter? The Statement gives several reasons:

1   It can assist in evaluating past stewardship of the company's resources by its management and thus the past performance of management. Such an evaluation can be helpful in informing predictions: while history may not repeat itself, managers who have shown themselves

to be good in the past are, perhaps, more likely to be able to perform well in future.

2   It can assist in assessing the company's capacity to generate cash flows from its existing resource base and the effectiveness with which its resources have been employed. Again this assessment is likely to be able to help in forming views about future effectiveness and cash flows, including the success with which additional resources may be employed.

3   By comparing outcomes with previous forecasts made by the investor or analyst, he or she may obtain feedback about the effectiveness of their forecasting model, sources of data, and so on.[2]

Financial position

According to the Statement,

> an entity's financial position encompasses the economic resources it controls, its financial structure, its liquidity and solvency, its risk profile and risk management approach, and its capacity to adapt to changes in the environment in which it operates. (SP, 1.15)

As with financial performance, the terminology does not conform to conventional accounting practice, but we can see that the sort of information envisaged here could be thought of as corresponding to what is to be found in the balance sheet: for example, 'economic resources' could be interpreted as assets and 'financial structure' as liabilities and equity (and, thus, gearing).

While, again, investors are not concerned directly with a company's financial position, information about it can help their forecasting in several ways. The return achieved from the use of resources can be related to the level of resources employed. Put in very simple terms, we can calculate a rate of return and thereby overcome some of the problems that arise in looking at absolute returns, such as the effect of scale. Thus, for example, if we know that a company achieved earnings of £20 million with resources of £80 million, we can calculate its return on capital as $20/80 = 25\%$. If we know that it has raised an extra £20 million of capital, we may feel confident that it will achieve the same return on the new capital and thus forecast its earnings for the following year as £100 million × $25\% = £25$ million.

Information about financial structure helps us to understand (a) how future cash flows will be distributed between parties with an interest in the company (in simple terms, gearing affects the distribution between interest and returns to shareholders); (b) past performance in managing capital requirements; and (c) future ability to raise capital. Liquidity and solvency affect the ability of the company to meet its debts as they fall due and thus continue to operate. Information about risk profile and risk management approach can assist in evaluating performance and position and in assessing the risk attaching to future cash flows. The issue of 'capacity to adapt' is relatively novel in financial reporting and we will discuss it a little later.

Generation and use of cash

As we have seen, cash flow plays a very significant role in determining a company's ability to pay dividends and thus its current and prospective value to its investors. Although, ultimately, investors want to forecast future cash flows, information about past flows is useful in the same ways as discussed earlier in relation to past earnings: it can feed into a forecast and, once the forecast period has elapsed, be used to compare with the forecast data to evaluate the forecasting model and data.

Cash flow information is useful in assessing liquidity and solvency, the relationship between cash flow and earnings, and financial adaptability. Different types of cash flow affect the future prospects of the company in different ways. For example, investment outflows occurring now increase the likelihood of higher inflows (from the investment) in future, whereas trading outflows may relate to past operations. Thus investors will want information about cash flows broken down between relevant categories, such as operations, investment and financing.

Financial adaptability

The concept of *financial adaptability* is not as common in the literature of financial accounting practice as the other terms used in this section. The Statement defines the term in the following way:

> An entity's financial adaptability is its ability to take effective action to alter the amount and timing of its cash flows so that it can respond to unexpected needs or opportunities. (SP, 1.19)

The concept is related to the more familiar notion of liquidity but focuses on the full range of sources and uses of cash. Thus financial adaptability comes from the ability, relatively easily and quickly, to raise and repay capital, obtain cash from disposing of existing resources without disrupting continuing operations (for example by selling financial investments not needed in the business), and improve cash flow from operations, for example by selling stock at reduced prices.

The need for companies to display financial adaptability follows from the degree of risk associated with business, and the riskier the business, in general, the more adaptable it is desirable for companies to be. Adaptability may have some cost attached to it, though. For example, by holding surplus cash in investments which can be sold rapidly, a company may earn a lower rate of interest than would be available from a less liquid investment; hence, companies may need to avoid greater adaptability than is appropriate to their circumstances and investors may need to evaluate their success in maximizing returns by avoiding excessive adaptability. In general, investors require information about adaptability to help them evaluate the risk associated with the returns on their investment: just as the company's cash flows influence the dividends it can pay (and thus the investors' returns), so the risk attached to the company's cash flows influences the risk attached to the dividends it pays.

Other information

The forecasting models investors might use can, in principle, require any sort of information and many do, in practice, incorporate information beyond that described above. The additional information may be company-specific (for example, it might be appropriate to build in information about the directors of the company, since they will influence its future performance), or relate to the wider context, such as trends within the sector generally. The Statement of Principles limits its scope to the financial statements but does not claim that the information needs listed cover all the requirements of investors and specifically says that information will also be needed from other sources.

Criticisms of the ASB's general approach

Assertions that financial statements should be designed to satisfy users' needs, or the particular needs of individual user groups, are normative claims, that is, claims about how the world *ought* to be, rather than empirical observations of the way the world *is*. As such, they are open for discussion rather than subject to empirical testing.

The principle that financial statements should be designed to satisfy the needs of some identified group or groups of users has commanded reasonably wide acceptance as a sensible starting point for a conceptual framework. The assertion that satisfying the needs of investors will also benefit the 'common interest' (SP, 1.11) of other users is an empirical claim and rather more problematic.

In general, it is true that most of the user groups listed by the Statement have an interest in the continued existence of the company: for example lenders want the company to survive long enough to repay the loan, customers may want to reorder or make a claim on a warranty, employees obviously want security of employment, and suppliers will prefer to have the opportunity of making further sales rather than losing such an opportunity. Even users who would prefer to see the company go out of business (for example, members of the public who believe it is damaging the environment) have a concern with continuity in the sense that they do not want it: that is, they are not indifferent to the continued operation of the company and they may be interested in forecasting its future to determine whether to step up protests, for example.

However, except in the case of lenders, there will normally only be a very limited degree of interest in the company and its business as a whole: for example, suppliers and customers will be mainly concerned with the specific unit or production line with which they deal, environmentalists will be concerned with whichever aspect of the company's affairs affects the environment, and so on. Further, the financial aspect of the company's affairs may be of only limited impact: for example, employees will also be interested in non-financial matters such as working conditions.

Hence, realistically, the information produced for investors cannot be seen as going very far to satisfy the information needs of most of the parties identified by the Statement of Principles as potentially users of financial statements. While the Statement of Principles' claim that investor-oriented information can satisfy the common interests of other groups is valid, this *common* interest may not in practice go very far to satisfy other groups' needs.

A further problem is that the information needed to make investment decisions may vary from one type of investor to another. For example, potential investors looking to buy a small number of shares in a large, multinational enterprise to add to a well-diversified portfolio may need different information from someone contemplating the purchase of a 50% share in a small local shop using the whole of their life savings. In the former case, for example, the potential risk is relatively low (only a small proportion of the investor's funds are involved, large institutional investors will monitor management, the existing portfolio offers some protection, and so on) whereas in the latter case it is high. If risk level is different, the need for information about risk may be different. Thus even settling on investors as the target user group does not eliminate the problem of differing needs.

If the ASB's approach fulfils the needs of investors better than it fulfils those of other groups, it would be possible to attack this position by arguing that investors already have advantages over other groups in society and should not be given further support, although whether reducing the usefulness of financial statements to investors would in fact benefit generally disadvantaged groups within society is at least open to question.

The rest of the framework discussed in this chapter, that is, both the claim that investors use financial statements and the – more complex – issues about the sorts of information they will find useful, is essentially empirical in nature. There is a body of empirical evidence about the use of financial information by investors and the relationship between share prices and accounting information that is growing rapidly in size and sophistication (for a useful summary, see Rees, 1995). The Statement of Principles makes no reference to this, preferring simply to make assertions about what will be useful, and this is to be regretted. The assertions in the Statement are, however, generally consistent with the empirical evidence and it has to be admitted that, as yet, there are few, if any, findings of a kind that can reliably be read across directly into a detailed specification of the information needed in financial statements (we will return to this point in Chapter 4).

Rees's survey of the relationship between share prices and accounting numbers concludes:

> the evidence . . . convincingly shows that:
>
> 1   Share prices and accounting earnings both measure some elements of the same characteristic and while the capital market is not omniscient, and the accounting measure of earnings is severely flawed, there is a considerable degree of agreement.
> 2   Although share prices and accounting earnings are strongly related, the capital market is largely able to pre-empt the delayed accounting disclosure.
> 3   Despite this, the accounting disclosure contains valuable information as shown by the reaction to disclosure, implying that new information is being brought to the market. (1995: 222)

The first of these conclusions provides some comfort that, in embracing orthodox financial reporting's concern with earnings, the Statement of Principles is heading along sensible lines. The second reminds us that it would be naive to suppose that analysts wait until the financial statements for a particular period are published before attempting to adjust the evaluation they made at the end of the previous period: in practice, of course, they are trying to beat their rivals and will continuously adjust their evaluations, based on indirect information (such as competitor company results if published earlier) and any advance information they can obtain from the company via, for example, briefings from management. Even if the actual publication of a set of statements had no impact at all on share price, because analysts had forecast the information they contained perfectly, the model used to prepare the statements would be important (because it would determine the information the analysts were forecasting) and publication would be significant, because it would confirm for the analysts that their forecasts were correct – the feedback value of information described earlier. However, the third conclusion suggests that, in fact, analysts do learn something from the publication of the financial statements.

Rees also concludes that the use made by analysts of financial statements is perhaps less extensive in practice than would appear from textbooks and surveys which ask analysts to describe what they do rather than observing them at work. On the whole, information gathered from other sources assumes greater importance (1995: 222). The evidence does, however, show that analysts do use financial statements: the issue is simply about the balance between different sources of information.

This point reopens the issue of the demarcation between the financial statements (in conventional terms, the profit and loss account, the balance sheet and the cash flow statement), the financial report (the overall package of information including the financial statements but also other material such as the chief executive's commentary) and other information sources. We have seen that the primary focus of the Statement of Principles is the financial statements. The Statement of Principles itself explains that financial statements have 'various inherent limitations that make them an imperfect vehicle for reflecting the full effects of transactions and other events' (SP, 1.8). These limitations include (a) the need to classify and aggregate and to allocate the effects of continuous operations to discrete periods; (b) the focus on financial rather than wider effects such as the success of research and development; and (c) the backward-looking orientation. As a consequence of these limitations,

some information on the financial performance and financial position of the reporting entity can be provided only by general purpose financial reports other than financial statements – or in some cases is better provided by such reports. (SP, 1.9)

Notwithstanding these limitations, financial statements are 'the principal means of communicating accounting information on an entity to interested parties' and they therefore 'carry much of the burden that is placed on general purpose financial reporting to meet [its] objective' (SP, 1.7). If the Statement of Principles was designed to derive a specification of the information needs of users starting purely from an identification of those users and empirical information about their needs, the argumentation set out here would beg the question of what those needs were. Put another way, our approach would be to find out what information was needed and then supply it, rather than setting up constraints beforehand and then asking what sort of information, within those constraints, we should supply.

The approach taken by the Statement of Principles in effect limits the sort of information that will be supplied in the financial statements because of 'inherent limitations' that actually reflect conventional reporting practice rather than any inevitable consequence of the nature of information (for example a future-oriented profit and loss account covering, say, forecasts for the next ten years, could in principle be prepared quite easily).

This approach means that, in effect, it is taken as given by the Statement of Principles that financial statements will continue to exhibit at least some of the general character they exhibit at the moment: the financial and historical orientation, the use of classification and aggregation, and so on. While a completely unfettered analysis, based only on first principles and taking nothing else as given, might have reached the conclusion that such a character is exactly what is required, the Statement of Principles simply did not conduct such an analysis and thus cannot say, one way or the other. As a consequence, the Statement can only be used to answer questions about the information to be put in a set of financial statements exhibiting this character. The approach is logically acceptable, but its limitations need to be borne in mind. It is probably politically the only approach that would be acceptable to the key players in the financial reporting arena: it offers the opportunity for evolutionary development rather than radical change and is thus much safer. It clearly will not satisfy those who would prefer a radical reappraisal of the issue of information needs or a holistic approach that integrates all types of information, or at least all types that emanate from the reporting entity.

Some commentators would go further still and argue that the purpose of financial reporting should be not to provide information for decision-making as such but to influence management behaviour. According to this argument, accounting standards should set out to motivate managers to behave in the best interest of some specified group, for example investors. Thus if there are two ways of accounting for a transaction and one method causes managers to work harder than the other in investors' interests, this one would be chosen. For example, expenditure on research can, in principle, be capitalized or written off in the year in which it is incurred. Capitalization would mean that it appeared on the balance sheet and might mean that managers would work harder so as to be seen to earn a return on the asset; expenditure written off is less visible. On this basis, capitalization might be required so as to motivate managers.

This approach is at odds with our normal view of measurement. An analogy might be setting speedometers to record faster speeds than those at which vehicles are actually travelling, in order to encourage drivers to slow down and thus drive more safely. Whether or not this piece of social engineering is desirable in itself, there is a clear danger that speedometers would lose their credibility as measuring instruments.

A further point is that, even if this approach to financial reporting were desirable, it is far from clear how it would be applied in the great majority of cases.

Information needs and conventional financial reporting

We have just seen that the Statement of Principles appears to have accepted as given that the overall character of the financial statements should not change. As we worked our way through the lists of information needs inferred by the Statement of Principles from the uses which investors make of information in the financial statements, we saw that the specifications of these information needs also matched, in general terms, the sort of information already supplied by conventional financial reporting. Put crudely, financial performance is captured by the profit and loss account, financial position by the balance sheet, cash generation and use by the cash flow statement, and financial adaptability by information from all three. This was not, however, taken as given but derived from claims about users' needs.

It is very difficult to imagine how a Statement of Principles that did not align with conventional practice, at least at this bedrock level, could achieve any kind of general acceptance. While it is possible that the authors of the Statement[3] cynically manipulated its logic to yield this outcome, and thereby achieve acceptability, and that the result would not have emerged from genuinely *a priori* theorizing with no thought to a premeditated outcome, such an accusation would be a little unfair. After all, the identification of the objective, users and uses of financial statements, though derived from first principles, does reflect a social process already in existence for a considerable length of time. If the bedrock foundation of that process, as actually conducted, had been failing to meet the objective inferred for it, what would this tell us? Perhaps society has tolerated, and paid for, accountants who for many years have been failing to deliver even at this most basic level; but an alternative explanation, with at least some plausibility, would be that some or all of the inferred objective, users and uses were wrong. Thus the match between the information specifications derived in the Statement from the objective, users and uses it identifies and the fundamental model of financial reporting actually in use at the moment may be interpreted as confirming the soundness of the approach adopted by the Statement of Principles.

Notes

1 Price/0.60 = 4, therefore price = £0.60 × 4.
2 This point is explained in greater depth in Chapter 3.
3 And the numerous other similar conceptual frameworks adopted around the world: see Chapter 1.

References

Arnold, J. and Moizer, P. (1984) 'A survey of the methods used by UK investment analysts to appraise investments in ordinary shares', *Accounting and Business Research*, 195–208.
Rees, B. (1995) *Financial Analysis*. London: Prentice-Hall.

Further reading

For an analysis which focuses on the heterogeneity of user needs, and on the position of preparers (which is largely ignored by the Statement of Principles), see N. Dopuch and S. Sunder, 'FASB's Statement on Objectives and Elements of Financial Accounting: a review', *Accounting Review*, 1980, pp. 1–21.

For an argument that the interests of society at large may not be maximized by focusing on the information needs of investors, see D. Cooper, 'Discussion of "Towards a political economy of accounting"', *Accounting, Organisations and Society*, 1980, pp. 161–6.

For a passionate statement of the argument that accountants should not allow their measurements to be influenced by social goals, see D. Solomons, 'The politicisation of accounting', *Journal of Accountancy*, 1978, pp. 213–25.

3

Qualitative Characteristics of Financial Information

The next stage in the development of the conceptual framework is to determine the qualities which accounting information should have if it is to satisfy the objective identified in the previous chapter. This part of the framework contains some principles which can be applied very widely: in general terms, much the same qualities are needed in any information designed to enable recipients to take decisions, whether it is financial accounting information, management information, legal information, or, indeed, information about how to travel to New York for a holiday or build an ocean-going yacht. Although the Statement of Principles starts at this level of generality, however, it takes the discussion further, to develop more specific qualities of particular application to financial statements.

Contemporary British financial reporting is subject to authoritative requirements concerning the quality of information in two forms:

1 The statutory requirement that the financial statements show *a true and fair view*.
2 The *fundamental accounting concepts* incorporated in SSAP2 and company law, which include two, *consistency* and *prudence*, that are essentially concerned with information quality.

By comparison, the conceptual framework's treatment of qualitative characteristics is much more fully developed and systematic. The relationship between the requirements that apply at the moment and those of the conceptual framework is examined later in this chapter.

The Statement of Principles' scheme identifies five principal qualities required of financial information. One of these, *materiality*, is a threshold quality, that is, all information provided should meet a minimum standard in this area but, once this threshold has been reached, the criterion plays no further part in the specification of the financial statements. In the case of the other four qualities, *relevance, reliability, comparability* and *understandability*, the greater the extent to which the quality is present the better. However, the Statement of Principles gives relevance a special position by requiring that, where choices have to be made between options that are relevant and reliable but mutually exclusive, the option selected should be the one that results in the relevance of the information package as a whole being maximised. (SP, 3.1)

We will consider each of the principal qualities in turn, but first it is sensible to examine the relationship between two of them in particular, relevance and reliability. In brief, information is relevant if it can be used in making the decisions users wish to make, and reliable if it actually depicts what it claims to depict. Both terms are used in a rather specialist sense and it is only possible to grasp the force of the conceptual framework's treatment of qualitative characteristics if the specialist meanings of the two terms, and thus the contrast between them, are understood. Implicit in the concept of reliability is an acceptance that financial statements set out to capture an 'underlying' reality, the transactions and other events that contribute to an entity's financial performance and position. In any particular case, accounting numbers can succeed in capturing an aspect or dimension of that reality with greater or less success. In order to test how well the numbers capture 'reality', we need to decide which dimension to test them against. The test being applied when we examine reliability is how well the numbers capture the dimension of the underlying reality that they *claim* to capture. We are *not* testing them against some dimension we think they ought to capture or even the dimension users think they capture: the test is simply whether the numbers live up to the claims made in the financial statements about what they measure.

It is important to appreciate that the way in which the term 'reliable' is being used here is rather narrower than the meaning it is sometimes given in everyday life. We sometimes refer to something as reliable if we can indeed rely on it for the purpose for which we intend to use it. For example, my car is reliable because when I turn the key it starts first time and gets me to where I want to go without breaking down. In the same way we might describe information as reliable if it enables us to get decisions right. But that is not the meaning of the term being employed here: in the terminology of the conceptual framework we should, under those circumstances, talk about the information being useful. To be useful, information must be both reliable (in the conceptual framework's sense) and relevant.

The way in which the terms 'relevant' and 'reliable' are used in the conceptual framework can best be illustrated by a non-accounting example. Assume I am intending to travel from London to Newcastle by train and need to decide when to arrive at the station. An important information input to my decision-making will be a railway timetable. However, the only timetable I have available is for last year's service. In the meaning given by the conceptual framework, this information is highly reliable, because it accurately describes the underlying situation it claims to describe, namely the times at which trains ran to Newcastle *last year*. Given the decision I am actually trying to make, it may seem surprising to call last year's timetable reliable, and it is worth reflecting on what it is about the conceptual framework's definition of reliability that makes the description appropriate.[1] However reliable the information, my problem comes because last year's times are not directly relevant to the decision I want to make, namely when to arrive at the station to begin my journey this year. Thus the timetable is reliable but not relevant.

Knowing that, in general, railway timetables do not change much from one year to another, I may choose to treat the timetable as an approximation to this year's times. Treated in this way, the information is highly relevant, but how reliable it is will depend on how much change there has actually been in this particular case. However, what has put the reliability of the information in doubt is my decision to treat it as an approximation to this year's times; as what it originally purported to depict, namely last year's times, it remains reliable.

The relationship between relevance and reliability, as defined by the conceptual framework, is so important that it is worth illustrating it by a second non-accounting example. Suppose we wish to spend an evening visiting public houses in the countryside around Canterbury. Our (non-drinking) driver does not know the area well and needs a map. We have a choice between an official map drawn to the highest standards by the national cartographic service showing roads, villages and churches, but not public houses, and a sketch map produced by one of our colleagues. The latter shows public houses, but was drawn from memory immediately on returning from a similar previous trip, and what's more a trip on which we know our colleague took at least one drink in every public house the group visited. We know that it is a general feature of English country life that many villages have at their centre both a church and a public house, so there is a reasonable chance that by navigating to a church we will also find a public house, but this cannot be guaranteed in every case. Thus we face a choice between information (the official map) that is reliable because it depicts what it claims to depict (roads, villages and churches) accurately but is of limited relevance (because it does not claim to depict public houses), and information (the sketch map) that is highly relevant (because it depicts public houses) but may not be reliable (because the circumstances under which it was prepared mean that it may not reflect the physical reality it claims to depict).

Relevance

The formal definition of relevance is as follows:

> Information is relevant if it has the ability to influence the economic decisions of users and is provided in time to influence those decisions. (SP, 3.2)

This definition draws on a key feature of the objective of financial reporting established earlier: information is provided to aid decision-making and is valued for its ability to do so. Note that relevance is defined by the *capacity* to influence decisions, not by whether or not it actually does so.

The Statement of Principles' discussion of relevance focuses on two characteristics, at least one of which information needs to have if it is to be relevant: *predictive value* and *confirmatory value*.

As we saw in the previous chapter, investors' buying and selling decisions essentially require an evaluation of an entity's capacity to generate financial surpluses and associated net cash inflows, since it is these that will determine the entity's ability to pay dividends and this ability to pay dividends that will, in turn, influence the price of the entity's shares. Future financial surpluses and associated net cash inflows will also influence a range of other factors in which users of the financial statements may be interested, such as capacity to repay loans and ability to provide steady employment. Users may, in addition, wish to evaluate other aspects of the entity's future, such as the way in which it will alter its productive capacity and thus the effect this will have on future employment.

The function of financial reporting is not necessarily to provide an evaluation of future earnings and cash flow, but rather to provide information on which investors can draw in making evaluations for themselves. The information provided to users and the evaluations they prepare may differ in two ways. The first concerns the period to which the information relates: often information about past events may be useful in forecasting future events. Thus financial reports containing past events may be highly useful to investors and others who are seeking to forecast the future.

The second difference concerns the nature of the information. There does not have to be a direct correspondence between the type of information provided and the type of information in the forecast. Thus, for example, information about an entity's current resource base (such as the quantity and age of its plant) may be useful in forecasting how well it will be able to adapt to changing conditions or overcome adverse circumstances and this forecast will, in turn, feed into a cash flow prediction. Hence information about one thing, quantity and age of plant, contributes to a forecast of another, cash flow.

Predictive and confirmatory value are interrelated because of the cyclical character of both the entity's earnings and cash generating processes and the investor's process of evaluation. As viewed from any given moment in time, the entity's future earnings and cash flow will depend on past events, which have contributed to its current resource base; present events, which will determine its short-term success and cash flow; and future events, which will obviously influence earnings and cash flow in the future. Clearly, the impact of past events on the entity's current position is something that has already occurred and could thus potentially be known with certainty and simply reported in terms of the current position. However, although the events have occurred, the entity itself may not know exactly how they have affected the current position (as with, for example, expenditure on research) or what aspect of this impact users wish to know about. Also, preparers may not be able to measure all aspects of current position with sufficient reliability. Hence, it may be sensible to report past events as such as well as reporting current position. Further, the past record may offer a good guide to future events.

At this given moment in time, users will evaluate past, present and future events on the basis of the information they have been given in the latest financial statements (as well as information from other sources). Their evaluation may include (explicitly or implicitly) earnings and cash flow forecasts, a forecast dividend stream, and forecast security prices, derived from the information they have been given. If the information they have been provided with is to be useful in this stage of the process it must have predictive value. In the words of the Statement of Principles, information 'has predictive value if it helps users to evaluate or assess past, present or future events' (SP, 3.3). It is worth emphasizing again that this does not mean that it must actually be a prediction, or that it must be in the same form as the required prediction so that a forecast can be obtained merely by extrapolating the time series. It is only necessary that the information contributes to the process of preparing the forecast by making the forecast better than it would be without the information.

As time passes, periods which were previously in the future and thus the subject of forecasts become past periods with known outcomes. There is a new resource base, the immediate future refers to periods which were previously more remote, and perhaps fresh periods previously too far off to need to be considered now have to be brought into the planning horizon. Users need to make fresh forecasts, based on a further round of financial information.

A second use of financial information now comes into play and we can identify a further reason for providing information about past periods, even though the purpose for which information is sought may be to make predictions. Users can compare the information they receive about what actually happened in the past with their own individual forecasts of what would happen and by doing so may learn something about the methods they are employing to make forecasts or the information to which they are applying those methods.[2] If events turned out as they forecast, this may suggest that their methods are sound; if events turned out significantly different from their forecasts, their methods may be faulty, although, of course, in any one instance it may simply be that some unusual circumstance that could not have been forecast has upset the usual pattern. By inspecting the size and direction of differences between forecasts and outturn, users may be able to improve their methods for the future. As the Statement of Principles puts it, 'information has confirmatory value if it helps users to confirm or correct their past evaluations and assessments' (SP, 3.3). Note that confirmatory value embraces not merely showing that a prediction was right but also showing that one was wrong.

It is worth illustrating confirmatory value by means of a simple example. Suppose that a year ago you were forecasting the earnings of a given company. You had outturn information for the three previous years:

	Earnings (£m)
19X1	20
19X2	25
19X3	30

By extrapolation (and ignoring compounding), it would appear that earnings for 19X4 might be in the order of £35 million, but you also know that the industrial sector in which your target company operates is expected to suffer a downturn in the year. Should you stick with a forecast of £35 million, reduce it to the same as 19X3, or perhaps reduce it further? Once the outcome for 19X4 is known, you can compare it with the forecast you arrived at, to learn something about how heavily your company is influenced by sectoral effects: for example if the sector, as a whole, does suffer a downturn but earnings of your company amount to £37 million, you might thereafter want to base future forecasts on the assumption that the company is not heavily influenced by sectoral factors.

In order, then, to be relevant, information must have either predictive value or confirmatory value or, of course, both. In principle, users could be provided with one set of information to make predictions and a different set to confirm past evaluations; in practice, however, it is likely that much information will be used for both purposes.

Obviously, in order to help with predictions, and thus decisions, information must be available in time to make the decision. *Timeliness* is treated by the Statement of Principles as a component of relevance.

Reliability

According to the Statement of Principles:

Information is reliable if:

(a)   it can be depended upon by users to represent faithfully what it either purports to represent or could reasonably be expected to represent;

(b) it is free from deliberate or systematic bias (i.e. it is neutral);

(c) it is free from material error;

(d) it is complete within the bounds of materiality; and

(e) in its preparation under conditions of uncertainty, a degree of caution (i.e. prudence) has been applied in exercising judgement and making the necessary estimates. (SP, 3.8)

Faithful representation

As explained earlier in this chapter, the Statement of Principles' approach to reliability takes it for granted that there is an 'underlying reality' which the financial statements are describing. One component of reliability is that users can depend on information 'to represent faithfully what it either purports to represent or could reasonably be expected to represent' (SP, 3.8). Put another way, the recognition, measurement and presentation of a transaction or other event should correspond closely to the actual effect of the transaction or event. The aspect of reality against which information is to be tested for this correspondence is determined by the claim inherent in the descriptions used in the financial statements and by what reasonable users would expect. Thus if the balance sheet contains under assets the entry 'Cash: £1 million', the description (the word 'cash') means that the item is claiming (purporting) to be the cash owned by the entity at the balance sheet date. This is a fairly straight-forward piece of reality to test: either the entity does indeed own cash resources to the amount of £1 million, so that the information is reliable, or it does not and the information is unreliable. The information will be unreliable if the entity owns less *or more* than £1 million; the claim is that the entity owns £1 million, not that it owns at least £1 million. Reliability is governed by the relationship between the accounting numbers and the underlying reality, not the damage done by the lack of correspondence.

Faithful representation is tested not only against the specific claim within the information itself about what is represented, but also against any other interpretation a user might reasonably make of what is rep-resented. Thus, for example, if a car dealer included its stock of vehicles under the caption 'vehicles' within the fixed assets section of its balance sheet, it would be in breach of the requirement for reliability because a user would, with good reason, expect those particular vehicles to appear in current assets under 'stock'. The need to check against users' expec-tations arises both where they may have expectations in addition to the claim made in the description and where that description is inadequate to identify the claim being made.

The nature of the underlying reality that financial statements seek to capture is not straightforward and this means the issue of faithful rep-resentation is itself problematic. Clearly, information may be unfaithful because it is erroneous in a fairly obvious way: a claim that the entity owned cash resources of £1 million when it actually had an overdraft of

£2 million and no cash would be recognized by most people as simply wrong (and probably fraudulent). However, information may be a less than completely faithful representation, not because it is erroneous in this way, but because of inherent difficulties either in identifying the transactions and other events the statements are seeking to capture or in devising and applying measurement methods and presentation techniques so as to portray those transactions or other events (or, of course, both). In some cases the problems may be such that there is no way of achieving an acceptable level of reliability and the information, however relevant, must be excluded from the statements. In other cases, it may be appropriate to include the items in the statements but disclose the nature of the problems surrounding their reliability. This issue is taken up in Chapter 5.

Complex transactions and other events may comprise a number of different rights and obligations, and the way in which they are accounted for will depend on the weight given to each in deciding the treatment; the way in which those given most weight are characterized; and how items are measured and presented. In order to achieve a faithful representation it is necessary to reflect the *commercial effect* or *substance* of the transactions or other events. This is achieved by identifying all rights and obligations but by giving greater weight to those that are likely to have commercial effect in practice and by accounting for and presenting transactions and other events in a way that reflects that commercial effect. When separate transactions or other events achieve, as a group or series, an overall commercial effect, they should be accounted for as a whole and not individually.

As the Statement of Principles points out (SP, 3.13), the legal form of a transaction or other event may be at odds with its substance; for example, as we shall see, something described in legal terms as a sale may have the commercial effect of a loan. The legal characteristics of a transaction or other event play an important part in determining the commercial effect of the event but do not define it because they have to be construed in the context of other characteristics.

This point, and the amount of space devoted to substance by the Statement of Principles, is best understood in the context of the history of financial reporting practice. A general requirement to reflect the substance of transactions was first introduced into accounting standards by FRS5 in 1994. For many years before then, it was often claimed that financial reporting followed a doctrine of substance over form but it is debatable whether this doctrine was properly applied except where law or standards required economic substance in specific instances. For example, one device employed historically to manipulate the financial statements was the construction of contracts so that legal ownership of a property passed from one entity to another but the risks and rewards normally associated with ownership remained with the first (the 'selling') entity. For example the first entity may continue to use the property and to take responsibility for maintaining and insuring it: it may even hold a matching contract to reacquire the property for a predetermined sum. The first entity may, of course, have received cash from the new owner on the 'sale' and have to make payments to the new owner in return for its continued use of the property or its return in due course, but it could be argued that the original cash receipt on the 'sale' was in commercial effect a loan and that subsequent payments are in the nature of repayments of the loan with interest: the cash flows involved would be the same. If substance over form is properly applied it is arguable that in this circumstance the first entity continues to hold the property, because it continues to employ it as a resource, and that the cash flows represent a financing arrangement, namely a loan. However, unless required to reflect commercial substance by specific accounting standards, it has historically been the case that entities have sometimes taken the opportunity to treat the initial transaction as a sale, thereby removing the property from the balance sheet: indeed deals have been structured precisely to make this possible. As a result the conceptual framework here underlines the importance of substance as a component of reliability.

Neutrality

The Statement of Principles defines neutrality as freedom from deliberate or systematic bias. If the reality beneath the financial statements was straightforward, there might be no need for a requirement for neutrality, in that information could be shown to be either right or wrong and in the latter case it would fail the faithful representation test. However the underlying reality is not straightforward and thus the representation may be less than perfect. As well as needing to ensure that the depiction corresponds as closely to the underlying reality as possible, we need to ensure that the 'gap' between depiction and reality is not systematically biased in one direction rather than another.

Consider an example. Suppose that colleges are funded by government on the basis of the number of students attending courses. The headcount takes place on some specified date. If the college is large there will always be some errors in the count: a student who left the college just before the count date may not have been removed from the register; a student switching courses may have been added to the register for the new course but not yet deleted from the old course; another student switching courses may have been removed from the register for the old course but not yet added to the new course; and so on. The funding agency is likely to accept that there will be errors in the count but to become concerned if, year after year, the errors always seem to produce a higher count (and thus more funds) and never a lower count.

As the Statement of Principles points out, financial statements are not neutral if information is selected or presented in a way that causes judgements, or the decisions based on those judgements, to take a pre-determined direction independently of the actual transactions or other events being represented. Continuing the example from the previous paragraph, the funding agency will be even more concerned if there is evidence of systematic practices designed to secure the upward bias in numbers – for example if students switching courses are always registered on the new course a month before they are removed from the old.

Accounting examples of possible bias leading to predetermined outcomes include the choice of accounting policies for depreciation with the intention of influencing the profit profile – for example the choice of straight line depreciation deliberately to increase profit in the earlier years of a new operation with relatively high capital expenditure in those early years, when other factors (for example the choices of similar entities) might have resulted in the use of reducing balance.

Completeness and freedom from error

Financial statements are highly aggregated and cannot show everything, but omitting relevant items or including errors can mislead and thus the Statement of Principles requires that information be 'complete and free from error – at least within the bounds of materiality' (SP, 3.16). Materiality itself is discussed later in this chapter.

Prudence

One of the ways in which the underlying reality that financial statements depict is problematic is that although what is depicted generally relates to the present, the need to reflect relevant attributes of present position, and in particular substance, means that the measurement process requires consideration of the future. Examples of the need to consider future events drawn from everyday contemporary reporting practice include:

1   Stocks should be written down to net realizable value if this is below cost – and net realizable value requires an estimate of a future event, namely the amount for which they will be sold.
2   Debtors should include only those amounts that will be collected – and this requires an estimate of whether individual debts will prove collectable.
3   Fixed assets with a limited economic life should be depreciated over that life – and this requires an estimate of what that life will turn out to be.

In the case of debtors, for example, it would be possible to provide a measurement based on legal form: that is, including all debts that are legally enforceable. However, if it will not in fact be possible to enforce a given debt, the debt will clearly not contribute to future cash flow and thus will not be relevant to users.

The need to make estimates of future events inevitably introduces a degree of uncertainty into the process of measurement and thus means that accounting numbers may turn out to be 'wrong' in the sense that future events turn out other than as forecast, for example a greater or lesser proportion of the legally enforceable debts outstanding at the balance sheet date may actually be collected. According to the Statement of Principles, the appropriate response to this uncertainty and the danger that the accounting numbers may be inaccurate, in this sense, is the disclosure of the nature and extent of the uncertainty and the exercise of prudence in drawing up financial statements:

> Prudence is the inclusion of a degree of caution in the exercise of the judgements needed in making the estimates required under conditions of uncertainty, such that gains and assets are not overstated and losses and liabilities are not understated. (SP, 3.19)

This means, among other things, that more confirmatory evidence of the existence of assets and gains and greater reliability of measurement are necessary before they are incorporated in the financial statements than is the case for liabilities and losses. Evidence and reliability of measurement are dealt with more fully in Chapter 5.

The Statement goes on to say that prudence is not needed where there is no uncertainty and that the exercise of prudence should not go as far as deliberately understating assets or gains or overstating liabilities or losses so as to create hidden reserves. 'Hidden reserves' is the term used to describe a situation in which the ownership interest is higher than disclosed in the financial statements. Consider, for example, the following published balance sheet:

	£m
Ordinary share capital	2.0
Profit and loss account	5.0
	7.0
Building:	
Cost (estimated life 20 years)	8.0
Depreciation (after 5 years)	2.0
	6.0
Current assets:	
Debtors	3.0
	9.0
Less current liabilities	2.0
	7.0

Suppose we know that the building is actually virtually certain to last 40 years (so that after 5 years the accumulated depreciation needed is £8.0m × 5/40 = £1.0m and not £2.0m), that debtors have been included after a provision for bad debts of £0.5m which is very unlikely to be needed, and that the figure for current liabilities includes a provision for claims against warranties on the entity's products of £1.5m, when in fact its products are so reliable that no customer has ever made a claim. Under these circumstances there are hidden reserves amounting to £3.0m and the balance sheet should show:

	£m
Ordinary share capital	2.0
Profit and loss account	8.0
	10.0
Building:	
Cost (estimated life 40 years)	8.0
Depreciation (after 5 years)	1.0
	7.0
Current assets:	
Debtors	3.5
	10.5
Less current liabilities	0.5
	10.0

The profit and loss account comprises £5.0m as before plus £3.0m previously hidden reserves. Such hidden reserves amount to deliberately biasing the owners' equity figure downwards and are thus inconsistent with the requirement for neutrality.

The Statement of Principles does not indicate whether the call to exercise 'a degree of caution' is to be understood psychologically, that is as a need for a particular attitude of mind in making estimates, or statistically, that is as a need to select appropriately from a range of estimates. A simple example serves to illustrate the difficulties of measuring items in a context of uncertainty.

Imagine that you are owed £10 million by a client who is in financial difficulties. You estimate that the likelihood of various possible outcomes is as follows:

Amount received £m	Probability
10	30%
5	25%
1	25%
nil	20%

The most likely single outcome is receiving the full amount but there is a 70% chance that including this in the balance sheet will overstate the amount actually received. There is a 55% chance that at least the amount that falls in the middle range of possible outcomes (£5m) will be received but there remains a 45% chance that this will turn out to be an over-statement. There is a 75% chance of receiving at least £1m, but a 55% chance that this will be a substantial understatement and a 30% chance that the understatement will amount to 90% in terms of the value actually received.

Comparability

Many of the methods used to interpret the information in financial statements involve making comparisons. Users may wish to compare:

1 An aspect of an entity's position or performance (for example, sales) through time (trend analysis).
2 One aspect of an entity's performance or position at a particular point in time with another aspect at the same time (for example, to calculate return on investment).
3 One or more aspects of an entity's position or performance at a particular point in time with the equivalent data for another entity, or with the average of all entities in the same class, or with some pre-established standard or norm. (These are all really variations on the same type of comparison because the point is to establish what is appropriate or reasonable or achievable by the entity in question by looking to an equivalent entity or the class of which the entity is a member or some authoritative judgement embodied in the norm.)

Although, in principle, users are seeking to compare the underlying realities of the various entities, they inevitably find themselves comparing the financial information itself, since this is the only way they have of getting to grips with the underlying reality. Everyday ratio analysis is an excellent example of methods requiring comparison but it should be borne in mind that comparisons are often less formal than ratio analysis and may simply involve a user looking across from one set of financial statements to another to get some intuitive feel of, for example, how large one entity is against the norm for the industry.
    To enable users to make comparisons,

> information needs to be prepared and presented in a way that enables users to discern and evaluate similarities in, and differences between, the nature and effects of transactions and other events taking place over time and across different reporting entities. (SP, 3.22)

It is easy to construct abstract examples to illustrate these notions. Consider three entities, A, B and C, operating in the biotechnology industry. Each has undertaken development work on a new project to the value of £10.0 million. Suppose the accounting standard applying to this type of activity permits such expenditure to be written off immediately or, subject to tests designed to ensure that the project will be successful, capitalized and amortized over future periods.[3] A and C write off expenditure while B capitalizes it. We happen to know that the projects of A and B are highly likely to be successful while C's project will not be. The balance sheet positions and the amount of development expenditure that will actually be successful in terms of delivering future profits are as follows:

	Carrying amount on balance sheet	Expenditure that will result in future profits
	£m	£m
A	nil	10.0
B	10.0	10.0
C	nil	nil

It is easy to see that A and B actually experienced similar events (expenditure which will yield future profits) but these are represented in dissimilar ways, while A and C experienced events which statement users interested in future cash flow would be likely to view as highly dissimilar (A will enjoy future cash flow, C will not) but have represented them in a similar manner (write-off).

Unfortunately it is not so easy to identify in practice all cases where representations are out of line with underlying reality. One reason why entities may be allowed a free choice between capitalization or write-off for certain sorts of expenditure is precisely the level of uncertainty associated with determining whether the expenditure has in fact been successful. In this example we have assumed away this level of uncertainty by taking the final outcome as known.

One valuable lesson to be learned from the above example is that merely imposing a single *uniform* treatment for all items in a given class will not necessarily achieve comparability. In this example requiring immediate write-off would have left A and B with similar underlying positions and similar balance sheets, though the correspondence between balance sheets and underlying reality would be questionable. However, the appearance of similarity in the balance sheets of A and C would mask highly relevant dissimilarity in their underlying positions. This lesson is often overlooked by those who would argue that all that matters in accounting standardization is to select one accounting policy and require every entity to follow it. The appearance of comparability this might offer to lay users is in fact misleading as the above example shows.

The contents of the Statement of Principles should enable standard-setters to determine how to account for classes of transactions and other events in the way that is, overall, most useful. Once standards have been established, preparers will enhance the comparability of financial statements by following them and in this way the standardization process can enhance comparability. It is important to understand that this enhancement follows from the validity of the standards in terms of qualities such as relevance and reliability and not merely from there being a uniform standard. If the standard was chosen arbitrarily (for example by tossing a coin) and then imposed on preparers, the resulting uniformity and appearance of comparability could, as illustrated in the previous paragraphs, be an illusion.

According to the Statement of Principles, comparability 'can usually be achieved through a combination of consistency and disclosure of accounting policies' (SP, 3.22).

Consistency

We have already seen that, to achieve comparability, like events must be treated in a like manner. Part of this 'treatment in a like manner' is measuring and displaying them in the same way, that is consistently. Consistency extends beyond matters of accounting treatment to issues about, for example, classification and display.

Suppose, for example, an entity regularly reports its operating costs in a manner distinguishing between manufacturing, distribution and administration costs. There may be an element of arbitrariness in classifying, for example, the payroll cost of the clerk at head office who deals with the administration of vehicle taxes: should this be included in distribution or administration? The principle of consistency argues that, at a minimum, whatever classification is adopted in one period should be followed in succeeding periods. If this is not done, erroneous impressions may be communicated by the financial statements. For example, suppose the profit and loss account in two successive periods included the following:

	First period £m	Second period £m
Distribution	9.0	10.0
Administration	1.5	1.0

This implies that distribution activity is increasing while the administration is being cut back. This impression would be misleading if the change in fact came about because £0.5m of expenditure classified as administrative in the first period had merely been reclassified to distribution in the second period.

In the previous section we saw that, though treating like events in a like way is necessary to achieve comparability, merely treating like events consistently will not achieve comparability if the treatment itself is inadequate or if other events, which are different in character, are also treated in the same way, thereby making them appear alike, and thus undermining the meaningfulness of the information even for those events which are appropriately treated. This is also true of the other aspects of consistency discussed here. For example, consistently including all administrative costs in 'distribution' and showing administrative costs as nil, or classifying administrative costs correctly but sometimes adding in costs of fixed assets that ought to be capitalized, will not yield comparable information.

Consistency is needed:

1   between like items in the same period for the same entity
2   in the same entity through time
3   between entities in the same period and through time.

There is a significant difference between the first two items in this list and the third. The first two can be achieved by the entity itself and could thus, in principle, be left to preparers. The third cannot be achieved by individual preparers and thus requires action at a higher level. So long as there is a need for type 3 consistency, there is a need for accounting standards, regardless of whether individual preparers can be relied on to choose policies appropriate to their individual entities.

Consistency, sometimes known as uniformity, can produce unreliable information. In the same way, consistency should not be used as an excuse for retaining a previously acceptable accounting policy that no longer provides the most useful information. This applies both to those cases in which an entity is selecting an accounting policy in an area that is not covered by an accounting standard, and to those cases where there is a standard permitting a particular policy but this policy is no longer appropriate. In such cases preparers who like the existing policy may be tempted to argue that it should be retained in the interests of consistency (with previous periods) but this argument is invalid. Of course, the disruption caused by a change in accounting policy, in terms of both comparability and the cost of instituting the new arrangements, is a valid reason for changing a standard only when it has been clearly demonstrated that the new policy is preferable, and this does introduce a degree of conservatism into the process that is entirely appropriate. The point here is that this degree of conservatism should not be extended to resisting change even in those cases where the net benefit from the change (after deducting the cost of losing comparability with previous periods) remains positive.

Disclosure of accounting policies

Users need to know that information is consistent or to be able to react appropriately to inconsistencies through time, between like transactions or other events, or between entities (for example, by adjusting data). The methods used by entities to apply accounting standards or account for transactions or other events where there is no applicable standard (that is, accounting policies) should be disclosed, as should changes in policies and the effect of such changes.

Understandability

Clearly, if users cannot perceive the significance of information they will not be able to use it appropriately. Understandability can be distinguished from relevance: if you are hungry but can eat only some sorts of food, a menu in a language you do not speak is not understandable but remains relevant because of its inherent qualities: you can use it by, for example, calling on an expert (someone who speaks the language in which it is expressed) to aid you in taking your decision. Understandability depends in part on characteristics of the information – the way items are aggregated, classified and presented – and in part on the capabilities of users.

The issue of the level of accounting ability that should be assumed in users of the financial statements is a crucial one in designing those statements. The statements with which the conceptual framework is concerned are the 'general purpose' statements designed to satisfy the needs of a range of users, though focusing primarily on investors (see Chapter 2). Users of such statements are likely to have a wide range of abilities, varying from the very limited skills of rank amateurs, with a small sum to invest and little time to carry out their investigations, to sophisticated investors and trained and experienced financial analysts, professionally employed to provide investment advice to institutions and wealthy individuals.

Clearly, users at the 'amateur' end of the spectrum will simply not be able to cope with the sort of complex and large-scale disclosures that users at the other end of the spectrum will want to receive. Their inability to cope will cause two sorts of problem. They may be unable to obtain any worthwhile amount of information from the statements because they simply cannot find their way round the reports, confused as they are by the volume of information, the complexity of its structure, the difficulty of the language needed to describe the disclosures, and the presentational methods and techniques (perhaps including graphs, ratios, and so on).

But suppose some way could be found of overcoming this problem? The statements might be structured in such a way as to communicate the 'basic' information that can be understood by naive users separately from other, more sophisticated material: indeed, a separate report might be issued for naive users (perhaps using a more delicate turn of phrase). Would this solve the problem? It might overcome the problem of potential confusion and 'information overload' for naive users but it would leave a second, perhaps more serious problem. The naive users would be trading in the same market as more sophisticated investors and yet would have less information on which to base their decisions. Under these circumstances they would arguably be handicapped and would find themselves always receiving the worst of the deal. This problem could, in turn, be solved by issuing to all users only the information that can be understood by naive users, but now we have two further problems: (a) sophisticated users are being denied information they need, so that the prices of securities are being set on the basis of less information than the market as a whole can handle and are thus, arguably, incorrect; and (b) the sorts of disclosures that can be required within the kind of framework that can be understood by naive users will themselves be restricted, so that preparers may be able to hide information that would be useful to all users.

The decision about how to resolve this dilemma is essentially a normative one (like that considered in Chapter 2 about what user groups to focus on). It is a policy decision to be made as a social choice by policy makers rather than following logically within the structure of the conceptual framework: in this way it is essentially part of the choice about user groups set out in Chapter 2.

The choice made by the Statement of Principles is described in the following passage:

> Those preparing financial statements are entitled to assume that users have a reasonable knowledge of business and economic activities and accounting and a willingness to study with reasonable diligence the information provided. (SP, 3.27(c))

Although not entirely clear-cut, this does imply that financial statements can assume reasonably sophisticated users. Naive investors should, perhaps, be warned that they may need to rely on expert advice or find other forms of investment.

Materiality

As explained in the introduction to this chapter, *materiality* is a threshold test: it is applied to see whether information that emerges from applying the other qualitative characteristics considered in this chapter is of sufficient significance to warrant inclusion in the financial statements.

Without this test, information that was relevant, reliable, and so on, but of no actual significance, could end up cluttering up financial statements unnecessarily. The test to be applied is as follows:

> An item of information is material to the financial statements if its misstatement or omission might reasonably be expected to influence the economic decisions of users of those financial statements, including their assessments of management's stewardship. (SP, 3.30)

Materiality is a function of the size and nature of the item, judged in the context of the case in question. The Statement of Principles sets out the main factors to be taken into account in determining materiality (SP, 3.31–32) but it is probably more useful here to consider a simple example. Suppose that a company's profit and loss account currently shows a profit of £10m for the period but that it is discovered that one transaction has been omitted from it. Should the statement be adjusted? Clearly, an important issue here will be size: if the transaction is an expense of £5m, thus halving the profit figure, it would seem to be material; if its value is only £100,000 (2% of the profit figure) it might not be thought to be material. But suppose that the transaction is for £100,000 and one of the following applies:

1   The transaction is a bonus payment to the chief executive.
2   It has been agreed that the managers will be paid a bonus if, but only if, profit reaches a minimum of exactly £10m.
3   The transaction is a bribe to a foreign customer which, if discovered, could result in the cancellation of a contract valued at £20m.

Under any of these circumstances the item might become material even though it would not be if it were a 'straightforward' trading transaction.

Trade-offs between qualitative characteristics

In practice, the nature of information generally is such that there will be conflicts between the various qualitative characteristics so that achieving more of one quality will reduce the level of one or more of the other qualities. Under these circumstances, it will be necessary to decide where to strike a balance between the pursuit of the various individual qualities. As the Statement of Principles puts it:

> On occasion, a conflict will arise between the characteristics of relevance, reliability, comparability and understandability. In such circumstances, a trade-off needs to be found that still enables the objective of financial statements to be met. (SP, 3.33)

We have already looked at some non-accounting examples of the conflict between relevance and reliability. A simple accounting example of such a conflict would be that reporting the amount legally owed to a company might be more reliable than reporting a figure adjusted for bad and doubtful debts, because the latter relies on an estimate: remember that reliability means that the information depicts what it purports to depict so that the figure for the amount legally owed to the company would be reliable if it accurately measured that sum. However, such a figure would be less relevant than the amount adjusted for bad and doubtful debts because it would provide a less accurate basis for determining the company's resource base and future cash flow. Thus there is a conflict between relevance and reliability.

The Statement of Principles says that where there is a conflict between relevance and reliability, 'it will usually be appropriate to use the information that is the most relevant of whichever information is reliable' (SP, 3.34). The test of relevance is applied to the information package as a whole (SP, 3.1).

The Statement's formulation can be interpreted as follows:

1   If at least one method produces information that clears a given minimum 'hurdle' level of reliability, employ from among those methods the one that achieves the greatest relevance, regardless of its relative reliability among those methods.
2   If no method produces information that clears the given minimum 'hurdle' level of reliability, choose on the basis of the trade-off between these characteristics.

This approach can be represented diagrammatically. Figure 3.1 shows the reliability of an information item on the horizontal axis and the relevance of the information package as a whole resulting from the inclusion of that item on the vertical axis. The level of reliability representing the minimum 'hurdle' to be cleared is shown by the thick vertical line: items to the left of this line are unreliable. There are four alternative methods of recognizing and measuring a given item (for example, four accounting policies) available, and the four information items that result from the application of these methods are shown by the points A, B, C and D.

Method A results in information that is unreliable. Since at least one method resulting in reliable information is available, it should not be selected. Method B results in information that is substantially more reliable, and only slightly less relevant, than methods C and D: nonetheless it should not be selected because, once the hurdle has been cleared, the objective is to maximize relevance regardless of the level of reliability. Methods C and D produce information that is more relevant than method B. Methods C and D produce information that is equally relevant, and therefore that producing the more reliable information, method D, should be selected.

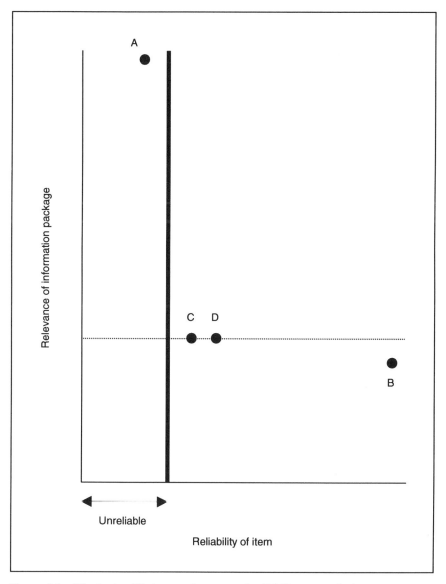

Figure 3.1   *The trade-off between relevance and reliability: example 1*

Figure 3.2 portrays a situation in which no method produces information that clears the hurdle of reliability. We can examine the position if the choice is between any pair of methods – that is, only two of the points labelled A, B and C are available. If the choice is between methods A and B, B should be selected because it is more relevant and more reliable (or, rather, less unreliable); if the choice is between B and C, B should be selected because it is as relevant and more reliable. However, if the choice is between A and C, we have no clear basis for making a

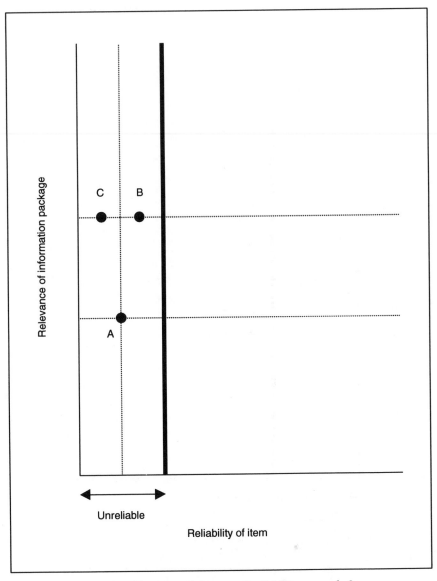

Figure 3.2   *The trade-off between relevance and reliability: example 2*

selection because one method is more relevant and the other more reliable.

Selecting among alternatives under these rules will nonetheless require the exercise of judgement since (a) the hurdle standard of reliability is not specified; (b) neither relevance nor reliability is capable of being measured with any precision; and (c) the need to make selections on the basis of the relevance of the package as a whole means that either the contribution to relevance from each item may differ according to the order in which choices are examined, or all choices for all items must be examined simultaneously – which can only be done in a 'broad brush' way.

One area in which the conflict between relevance and reliability commonly arises is the question of timeliness: on the whole, delaying the supply of an item of information until all the uncertainty associated with it has been resolved (for example, reporting the debtor balance only after all debts have either been paid or become known for certain to be uncollectable) increases the reliability of the information but may considerably reduce its relevance because it has simply become too late to make any use of it. The Statement of Principles requires that financial information should be made available as soon as, but not before, it is reliable.

There is also a potential conflict between two aspects of reliability, neutrality and prudence. According to the Statement of Principles,

> when there is uncertainty, the competing demands of neutrality and prudence are reconciled by finding a balance that ensures that the deliberate and systematic understatement of gains and assets and overstatement of losses and liabilities do not occur. (SP, 3.36)

However, in a world in which the measurement of items in the financial statements is far from unproblematic, the difference between exercising a degree of caution to ensure that, for example, assets are not overstated, and avoiding systematically understating them, is a subtle one.

Finally, the Statement underlines the notion that the preparation of financial statements should assume users of reasonable sophistication by indicating that

> information that is relevant and reliable should not be excluded from the financial statements simply because it is too difficult for some users to understand. (SP, 3.37)

The qualitative characteristics and contemporary practice

There are several aspects of contemporary GAAP that bear on the quality of information included in the financial statements. Two of these can be directly identified in law and accounting standards and these are considered in this section. The third, the doctrine of substance over form, has already been discussed.

The true and fair view

The annual financial statements of UK companies are prepared to comply with UK company legislation and are required by that legislation

a true and fair view'. The meaning of this phrase is far from
matic: many commentators are prepared to say forcefully what,
in their view, the phrase means but their interpretations do not coincide
and in some cases conflict. Since it is a legal test, the responsibility for
applying it ultimately rests with the courts, but this is of little help when
few cases reach the courts and those that do provide only limited
guidance in specific areas. The elusiveness of the concept has caused
more than one commentator to describe it as a 'will-o'-the wisp' (see
Parker and Nobes, 1994: 13).

Whatever one may make of it, however, the concept clearly occupies
an important place in contemporary UK financial reporting practice.
How is the use of the Statement of Principles to design accounting
standards going to square with the requirement that the resulting financial statements should show a true and fair view? The Statement explains
that it has the true and fair view concept 'at its foundation' (SP, Introduction, paragraph 13) and that this is evidenced by, among other things,
the Statement's employment of the qualities of relevance and reliability.
According to the Statement, true and fair is a dynamic concept and will
not be satisfied unless financial statements contain information of sufficient quantity and quality 'to satisfy the reasonable expectations of the
readers to whom they are addressed' (SP, Introduction, paragraph 12)
and these expectations will, themselves, change through time. The ASB
both responds to these changes and seeks to influence them by its
pronouncements, which will, in turn, be driven by, among other factors,
the Statement of Principles.

Thus the Statement of Principles is held both to conform to true and
fair and to be able to flesh out and change true and fair via its effect on
standards. On the other hand, the Statement indicates that it does not
'define the meaning of true and fair' (SP, Introduction, paragraph 13). In
summary then, according to the Statement, its conceptual framework is
consistent with and will help to develop the true and fair concept. It is
very difficult to prove or disprove this claim, not least because of the
elusiveness of the true and fair concept itself.

Fundamental accounting concepts

SSAP2 sets out four fundamental accounting concepts, of which two,
consistency and *prudence*, bear on the quality of accounting information.
These are also embodied in company law requirements applying to
financial statements.

The consistency requirement in company law is that accounting
policies should be applied consistently from one period to the next (CA,
Fourth Schedule, paragraph 11). SSAP2 requires that 'there is consistency
of accounting treatment of like items within each accounting period and

from one period to the next' (paragraph 14). In both cases, consistency is required in its own right and there is no reference to a requirement for comparability. As we have seen, the Statement of Principles relegates the role of consistency to being a component of comparability, with comparability being desirable in itself and consistency being a necessary but not a sufficient condition for comparability. Indeed, the Statement points out that there will be occasions on which consistency must be sacrificed, such as when a superior method of accounting becomes available. In practice, it has never been the case that once an accounting policy or treatment has been adopted it has been regarded by accountants as frozen in place for all time, so the Board is probably justified in saying that its notion of consistency is 'a more precise description' (SPED 1999, B3.11) of current practice, notwithstanding the way in which consistency is actually described in SSAP2 and the law.

The change in approach to prudence is more dramatic. Company law requires that the financial statements be drawn up on a prudent basis (CA, Fourth Schedule, paragraph 12). Neither SSAP2 nor company law define the term but both indicate that it requires that profits should be included in the profit and loss account only when realized and that all liabilities are recognized. It is not immediately apparent that this approach differs from that of the Statement. However, as the Board recognizes (SPED 1999, B3.6), the traditional approach to prudence essentially accepted that overstating losses and liabilities and understating assets and gains was, provided it was not carried too far, acceptable, and perhaps even desirable as a contribution to achieving prudence. The Statement's discussion of prudence, especially combined with the inclusion of the neutrality component of reliability, moves away from this to give much greater attention to providing unbiased information, so that the exercise of caution in making judgements does not result in deliberate and systematic understatement of assets and gains or overstatement of liabilities and losses.

The Board has explained that this development in thought since the adoption of SSAP2 is a response to increasing concern that smoothing reported profit, that is deliberately understating profit in 'good' years so as to create a hidden margin which can be released in 'bad' years to mask the real reduction in profit in those years, is as unacceptable as imprudent exaggeration of gains and assets (SP, Appendix III, paragraph 21). This position follows from the concern with providing relevant information to users who are attempting to evaluate the future potential of the entity: inaccurate data about the past are unlikely to enhance the quality of predictions. Sophisticated users do not need to be 'protected' from learning about the peaks and troughs of a company's performance because they can understand the patterns and react appropriately to them. If they are misled by financial statements which understate assets and gains, share prices will be set too low: this may benefit buyers but sellers suffer – and eventually everyone is a seller.

The development in the approach to prudence in the Statement of Principles reflects similar thinking in the other conceptual frameworks developed elsewhere and described in Chapter 1.

The ASB has issued an exposure draft (FRED21) that will supersede SSAP2 and bring accounting standards into line with the Statement of Principles in areas relating to the qualitative characteristics, including consistency and prudence.

Criticisms of the scheme

The Statement of Principles' scheme gives a narrative explanation of the qualitative characteristics of financial information to be pursued and some indication, however incompletely formulated, of the way in which conflicts between the characteristics are to be resolved. Both the definitions of the qualities and the framework for resolving conflicts are expressed in generalized and abstract terms. As such, they help to focus and move forward the debate about the specification of financial statements but do not provide an operational mechanism for dealing with concrete problems, including, for example, the need to establish trade-offs between the various qualities and components of those qualities (for example, prudence versus neutrality). These will continue to have to be dealt with by judgement in individual cases and whether or not the scheme will be of assistance at this level remains to be seen.

Some conceptual frameworks, including that developed in the USA, have incorporated within the scheme of qualitative characteristics a cost–benefit constraint requiring that for information to be reported, it must pass the test of yielding a greater benefit than the cost of providing the information. The Statement of Principles does not see this as a quality of financial information itself but lists cost–benefit as one of the factors that the ASB takes into account in setting standards (SP, Introduction, paragraph 14). Whether seen as part of the framework or as a factor to be taken into account in applying it, cost–benefit is an important feature of the standard-setting process. The benefits from improvements in financial information flow through primarily to the users of the information (in terms of better decisions), though there may also be social benefits from improvements in the allocation of resources and in spurring managers to improve performance. The costs of reporting improved financial information include any incremental resources used to generate and audit the new information compared with what was previously reported; any incremental resources used in disseminating the information (a substantial amount of new information might, for example, require the inclusion of an additional page in the annual report, with consequent possible increases in postage and so on); potential damage to the reporting entity's commercial position because competitors will also be able to obtain the information; and the costs involved in absorbing and analysing the new information (including the one-off costs of coping with the change).

A key consideration in applying both the qualitative characteristics and the cost–benefit criterion outlined above is that different users, even within a single user group, will have different characteristics and will thus, in principle, seek different rates of trade-off between the qualities and a different balance between costs and benefits. For example, a sophisticated user may be able to make good use of a relatively complex (and expensive) new disclosure and be happy to see the company incur the cost of providing it; while a less sophisticated user who cannot fully use the information in the new disclosure may prefer that the cost of providing it is not incurred, thus, for example, increasing company profits and hence her or his dividend. Again a highly risk-averse user requiring a very high standard of reliability might want different information to a less risk-averse user. In practice, of course, the ASB has to arrive at an overall decision on behalf of all users and of society at large, based on a judgement which must be highly subjective and intuitive.

The Statement's use of prudence has attracted some criticism. Some commentators feel that it does not go far enough to assert the importance of providing unbiased information and thus attaching as much importance to avoiding the understatement of profit as its overstatement. For others, the traditional approach is to be preferred:

Prudence [as defined by SSAP2] is a mainstay of traditional practice. The prudence concept creates an essential bias . . . a potent antidote to counteract preparers' eternal optimism. (Davies and Davies, 1996: 89).

Notes

1 Of course, as any traveller knows, a railway timetable may not be reliable even in this sense, but that is not the point being made here.

2 It will generally be impossible, strictly speaking, to evaluate the information and models separately. We also need to bear in mind that, in a social context such as the business world, our forecasts may themselves change future events (for example, if users forecast bankruptcy and seek to withdraw their investments, an entity may fail when it would not have done so if a different forecast had been arrived at).

3 The requirements of the standard actually applying in the UK are discussed in Chapter 4. This standard does not overcome the problems of comparability described here.

References

Davies, M. and Davies, P. (1996) 'The ASB's new principles for old', *Accountancy*, March: 89.
Parker, R.H. and Nobes, C.W. (1994) *An International View of True and Fair Accounting*. London: Routledge.

Further reading

For a critical analysis of qualitative characteristics in the context of the development of the Statement of Principles, see M. Page, 'The ASB's proposed objective of financial statements: marching in step backwards? A review essay', *British Accounting Review*, 1992, pp. 77–85. Note that this discusses an earlier draft of the Statement.

For a discussion of qualitative characteristics in a US context, see D. Solomons, *Making Accounting Policy: the Quest for Credibility in Financial Reporting*, Oxford: OUP, 1986, Chapter 5.

For a defence of the possibility and importance of representational faithfulness, see D. Solomons, 'The politicisation of accounting', *Journal of Accountancy*, November 1978, pp. 213–25.

For an alternative perspective on qualitative characteristics, see E. Stamp, 'Accounting standards and the conceptual framework: a plan for their evolution', *Accountant's Magazine*, July 1981, pp. 216–22.

4

Elements of Financial Statements I: Assets

We have now seen how the Statement of Principles identifies the objective of financial statements (Chapter 2) and establishes the qualitative characteristics financial information should possess if it is to satisfy that objective (Chapter 3). These two stages in the development of the Statement of Principles are expressed in fairly general terms: they provide a valuable analysis of the issues to be addressed when specifying the content of financial statements without taking us very far towards actually constructing such a specification. The third stage involves defining the elements which should be included in financial statements, and this moves us on to examining concrete issues, the resolution of which directly shapes the output of the financial reporting process.

The role of element definitions

According to the Statement of Principles, the *elements* of financial statements are 'the building blocks with which financial statements are constructed – the classes of items that financial statements comprise' (SP, p. 45). The financial reporting process should be designed to reflect in the financial statements the effects of the transactions and other events on the entity's financial performance, financial position, generation and use of cash and financial adaptability, in the way that provides the best trade-off between the qualitative characteristics required of those statements. An important aspect of the financial reporting process is the way in which the effects are classified and aggregated. The Statement of Principles regards the element definitions as imposing order on the financial reporting process by specifying how the classification and aggregation is conducted.

The definition of elements begins the crucial task of specifying the structure and content of financial statements. As we shall see, under the Statement of Principles, items which do not satisfy the definition of one or other of the elements cannot be included in financial statements: hence the system of definitions plays a crucial role in determining the *content* of financial statements.[1] In addition, the system provides the basic *structure* for statements because the items included in statements are grouped by element.

The notion that financial statements should be useful could be employed in addressing questions about the design of financial statements in a variety of ways. One approach would involve direct empirical investigation of the relationship between the objective of financial statements and alternative accounting policies available for use. It might be possible, for example, to set up experiments to measure whether capitalizing or writing off intangibles such as brands provides the more useful profit measure in taking decisions about buying or selling shares. This approach has indeed been advocated in general terms (see, for example, Carsberg et al., 1977) but there are very considerable difficulties in carrying out the necessary empirical tests. Different users may use the information in financial statements in different ways: for example they may use different statistical models to predict future performance. Hence it is difficult to determine how a given difference in the accounting numbers (for example the difference caused by capitalizing or writing off intangibles) will affect users' decisions and thus their subsequent gains from buying or selling the entity's shares. Furthermore, there are a great many choices available in drawing up a set of financial statements (taking into account all the items for which accounting policies are necessary), and unless they can all be tested simultaneously, the results will be affected by the order in which the alternatives are adopted. As a result, the approach has not been fruitful in practice (see Bromwich, 1989).

Alternatively, users of financial statements could simply be asked how financial statements should be designed, on the assumption that users are the best judges of their own needs. Such an approach has been adopted in numerous studies of what *types* of information should be disclosed. The results have, on the whole, been of limited use. Where users are offered a range of items of information they tend to ask for all the items suggested, or, if they are offered a great many items, some of them obscure, they will ask for all the items with which they are familiar. Any particular study will, of course, identify a few items at the top of the ranking but there is no solid basis for believing that the same items would be chosen by a different group of users or by the same group at a different time. The approach is condemned by its critics as the equivalent of asking children to make choices in a sweet shop: both children and financial statement users would, of course, like some of everything. The approach also disregards the cost of supplying large quantities of information and there are theoretical arguments against relying too heavily on the views of users. These include the consideration that users are likely to be excessively influenced by what happens to be already available or under discussion, because that is what they are familiar with, when an alternative and fresh model might yield better results (see

Sterling, 1970). The weakness of this approach in addressing the relatively straightforward question of what items of information should be included in financial statements is exacerbated when more complex issues, for example of structure and measurement, are addressed.

The approach actually taken by the Statement of Principles is rather different and does not rely on any empirical investigation of users or the financial reporting process. Rather it attempts by logical argument to deduce what should be included in financial statements given the objective and desirable qualitative characteristics it has previously identified. This approach has the enormous advantage that it can ignore the difficulties involved in empirical investigation of the very complex relationship between individual accounting numbers and the satisfaction of the objective of financial reporting; it suffers, however, from the disadvantage that it does not empirically demonstrate the existence of the linkage it claims to identify between the objective of financial statements and the prescriptions it offers, leaving it open to others to claim that other logical linkages are equally valid.

The Statement of Principles' system of element definitions is *comprehensive*. That is, under the Statement's system, the financial statements are made up of those elements identified in the system *and only those elements*: there are no other elements (and nothing can be included in the financial statements that is not an element). Thus nothing that falls outside the system of definitions can, according to the Statement of Principles, be included in the financial statements.

At the heart of the system is the definition of the element *assets*. All other element definitions are derived from the definition of assets. In the balance sheet, *liabilities* are the mirror image of assets and *ownership interest* is assets less liabilities. Flows between the entity and the rest of the world are, in turn, defined in terms of changes in ownership interest: increases in ownership interest comprise gains and contributions from owners, and decreases in ownership interest comprise losses and distributions to owners. Thus all other element definitions are derived directly or indirectly from the definition of assets. This is an important feature of the Statement and represents a great source of conceptual integrity while at the same time attracting a number of criticisms.

The character of the Statement of Principles' system of definitions, specifically that it is comprehensive and that all definitions are interrelated, means that the system resembles contemporary financial reporting practice in two key ways:

1   The inclusion of an item in the financial statements automatically requires the inclusion of another, 'balancing' item. For example the inclusion of an asset must be accompanied by the inclusion of a liability, a decrease in another asset, a gain or contribution from owners, or some combination of these. Thus the normal requirements of double-entry bookkeeping are satisfied.

2   The balance sheet and statement of financial performance *articulate*: that is, in overall terms, flows between the organization and the rest of the world recognized in any period account exactly for the net change in resources available to the entity between the beginning and end of the period, as recognized in the entity's balance sheets.

We have already seen that some central features of the Statement of Principles resemble contemporary practice and discussed various reasons why this might be so. The character of the system of element definitions is another respect in which the Statement of Principles resembles contemporary practice and the same possible explanations apply.

The nature of assets

The Statement of Principles defines assets in the following terms:

> Assets are rights or other access to future economic benefits controlled by an entity as a result of past transactions or events. (SP, 4.6)

The first and most important feature to notice about the definition is that it is expressed in economic terms: an item can be an asset only if it yields future economic benefits. This focus is derived from the approach to users and their information needs set out earlier in the Statement. Users need to be able to evaluate an entity's ability to generate future surpluses and associated net cash inflows (including the timing and risk involved). One important factor in determining ability to generate future cash flow is the level of resources under the command of the entity at any given point in time. In this context, the 'things' entities have (items) count as *resources* if they will yield future economic benefits, that is (a) cash, (b) other items equivalent to cash, or (c) the opportunity to avoid a decrease in cash available to the entity which would otherwise occur. Thus, to assist users to evaluate the cash generating potential of the entity, the statement indicating command over resources (the balance sheet) should define those resources in terms of ability to contribute to cash generation.

The linkage between the definition of assets and the overall objective of financial reporting is so simple to state that it can easily be ignored or taken for granted in a way that overlooks its power. Yet it is a vital aspect of the Statement of Principles: it offers a defence of the Statement as a means of improving financial reporting and contributes to its power as a practical tool for shaping financial reports. Perhaps the most important value of the Statement is in reminding us (a) that the form of financial statements should follow their function; and (b) what that function is. It is the derivation of the definitions from the prior statement of the objective of financial statements that should discourage the use of the system of definitions in a legalistic or excessively technical way that looks only at the bare words of the definitions.

Of course, in order to contribute to the cash generation of the entity it is necessary for resources to have other characteristics in addition to the ability to yield future economic benefits. First, the economic benefits must be going to flow specifically to the entity, so that resources benefiting other entities only or the world at large (with no particular benefit to the entity under consideration) will not qualify as assets of the entity. Secondly, the benefits must be under the control of the entity at the date of the balance sheet. These characteristics are discussed further below.

Although an economic approach to the definition of assets may seem the obvious one when viewed in the context of the Statement of Principles, it is not the only approach that has been taken by accountants. Historically, definitions of assets have tended to focus on the legal dimension as much as the economic. The following, which comes from a well-known guide to financial reporting published in 1988, is a good example of such a definition:

> Any property tangible or intangible from which future benefits are expected, and of which a company has a legal right of use as a result of a past or present transaction. (Parker: 111)[2]

By focusing on 'property' and legal rights, the definition would appear to exclude items which the entity controls by means other than legal rights. The definition quoted here is a hybrid and does require that there should be future benefits: a strictly legal approach would include as assets property which the entity had the legal right to use but which would not in fact yield future benefits.

Attributes of assets

Future economic benefits

Economic benefits are, in essence, received in the form of the consumption of scarce goods and services. Goods and services which are available freely, either because nature provides them in abundance (such as the air we breathe) or because society makes them available without charge (such as the framework of law and order within which entities function), are not scarce and thus cannot qualify as assets. Assets can arise when the consumption of goods and services will be possible at some point in the future. In this context 'the present' is a point in time rather than a phase: the benefit can become available one second after the balance sheet is drawn up but will still represent a future benefit at the balance sheet date.

The approach of the Statement of Principles is that, to represent an asset, future economic benefits have to be embodied in an *item*. The most obvious item potentially qualifying as an asset is cash held at the balance sheet date. Cash embodies future benefits because it represents the power to purchase (and thus consume) goods or services at any point in the future. The goods or services may be purchased and used by the entity to generate further benefits for its owners or the cash may be distributed to owners (for example, as a dividend), thereby enabling them to benefit from purchases of goods and services for themselves.

Even cash may not necessarily embody future economic benefits, for example if it is in a foreign currency which cannot for legal or other reasons be exchanged into one that can be spent in a part of the world to which the entity has access. Such a situation can arise when one country is subject to sanctions by the rest of the world, perhaps because of its human rights record.

Some of the items held by an entity represent the right to *receive* cash, which can then be used in the way discussed in the previous paragraph. Such items include trade and other debtors and repayable loans to third parties. These items can embody future economic benefits because there will at some point in the future be a transfer of cash to the entity, and that cash will itself then be available to acquire goods and services for consumption.

At one stage further removed from cash are the items which the entity holds to sell. These will in due course be traded in return for cash or for another item (generally a legally enforceable debt) which itself will be converted into cash.

Many items held by an entity will not be directly traded, but are available for use in producing other items which will be traded. This category includes not only many types of fixed asset but also current assets which are transformed in the production process into final products available for sale, such as raw materials and fuel. The chain leading through to the ultimate economic benefit is now growing rather lengthy (conversion, sale, receipt of cash, expenditure of cash) but it is still clear and unbroken and it is important that it is understood that it is this chain that can justify treating, say, a building as an asset. A building is not automatically an asset if it will not generate future benefits.

Although cash or the expectation of receiving cash will normally provide the future economic benefits underpinning an asset, it is not strictly necessary for there to be a prospective cash receipt to justify treating an item as an asset. The future economic benefit may take the form of a *reduction* in the cash outflow that would occur but for the existence of the item: a reduced future outflow is the economic equivalent of an inflow. This is the rationale for treating a debtor balance as an asset when the benefit will be received by deducting the amount from a larger sum that the entity owes to the debtor (or, indeed, to some other party that will accept an offsetting arrangement).

A further case in which there is no prospective cash receipt to the entity can arise. There may be non-cash goods (including claims to other non-cash goods or future services) which will never be converted into cash by the entity, even indirectly by use in a future production process. An example would be an entity established to drill for oil, on the basis that the oil found would not be sold for cash but would be distributed to the owners of the entity. The production platform will never generate cash but it, together with the stock of oil held by the entity at any given moment, can be assets. The production platform will, in economic terms, be converted into a stock of oil, and stocks of oil can be assets because they can be distributed to the owners in a transaction that will avoid the cash payment that would be necessary to transfer the equivalent value. In other words, to pay a dividend of, say, £1 million would normally require cash of that amount but in this case can be achieved by distributing oil of the same value. Hence ownership of the oil has saved the entity cash and thus generated a benefit.[3]

Because most items qualifying as assets fall into a limited number of descriptive categories (for example cash, debtors, stock and property) and most items falling into those categories qualify as assets, there is a tendency in practice for accountants to skip the process of testing items and to treat anything falling into the categories as assets automatically. The definition in the Statement of Principles reminds us that there must ultimately be future economic benefits for an item, even one falling within one of the standard categories, to qualify as an asset. We have already seen that cash itself may not be an asset if it is held in a form that prevents the receipt of future benefits. It is worth looking at another example, to underline this point.

Suppose a company operating on a large site has constructed, at a cost of several million pounds, a building designed to house new production capacity. A downturn in the economy means that demand for the product has fallen and it is not now economically justifiable to purchase the machinery needed to establish the production line. The building is in the middle of the company's site and there is no feasible means to sell or let it. The company has sufficient general storage on site already. The property falls into the category of land and buildings; it is legally owned; it is the consequence of past expenditure; but it is not an asset.

Access

In order that any entity can control future economic benefits, those benefits must exist in a form which is associated with rights to receive them or some other way of ensuring access to them. The expectation that benefits will arise is not, in itself, enough to indicate that an asset exists. For example, there may be a widespread belief that a local authority is about to create a new tourist attraction in a particular area and that this will result in an increase in visitors and an opportunity to establish profitable new businesses, perhaps selling refreshments and so on. In general, though, the benefits that are predicted cannot give rise to assets for any entity because no entity will have rights over, or other access to, them. This is because if the authority does, ultimately, decide not to establish the tourist attraction, or to establish it elsewhere, no entity will be able to stop it or claim compensation.

By far the most common way in which access to future economic benefits is established is by legal ownership of the property or other tangible or intangible item embodying those benefits. Legal ownership generally enables an entity (a) to use its property in the production of its own output; (b) to sell the property to a third party and obtain benefits in the form of the proceeds from the sale; or (c) to use the property to generate benefits in other ways, such as leasing a vehicle on to another party, granting licences to exploit a technical process or offering an investment as security for a loan.

Sometimes legal rights spring from some arrangement other than outright ownership. One example here would be an entity leasing a vehicle from a supplier: the lessee acquires legal rights under the contract to use the vehicle provided it meets its own obligations under the contract, such as making the rental payments as they fall due. Another example would be the right to manufacture and sell a product for which a third party held the patent, under licence from the owner of the patent. Again, the entity acquires the legal right to exploit the patent provided it meets its own obligations under the licence, which will normally include making royalty payments. Often the economic substance of these arrangements will differ little from those that arise in a straightforward case of ownership.

Though it is comparatively rare in practice, assets can exist in the absence of any legal rights and that is why the definition includes the phrase 'or other access'. An unpatented invention or a product made to an unusual ingredient list can give rise to an asset where it is possible for an entity to establish access to the future economic benefits, for example by keeping the details needed to exploit the invention or product secret. If the product specification can be used freely by other entities, for example because a secret recipe has been stolen and there are no legal rights to restrict its use, or because the state decides that information should be derestricted in the public interest, perhaps because the product is of great benefit to public health, the entity making the invention will have no access to benefits and thus there will be no asset.

The definition of assets emphasizes that the future economic benefits and the item embodying those benefits are to be considered separately. The asset is not the item itself but rather the future economic benefits embodied in it. A *single* item can give rise to more than one asset if the future economic benefits can arise in more than one 'bundle': this is easiest to understand where different entities hold the rights to the different bundles. To take a simple, but rare, example, suppose two separate entities purchase a single van with a legally watertight agreement that one entity will use it between Monday and Wednesday and the other from Thursday to Saturday. On the definition in the Statement of Principles, this is not joint ownership by the two entities of a single asset, the van: rather we have two separate streams of economic benefits (deriving from the use of the van in the first and second half of the week respectively), each of which can qualify as an asset for the relevant entity.

While it may appear overly precious to argue in this context about whether we have joint ownership of a single item of property or separate access to two bundles of future economic benefits, such issues do affect the shape of the financial statements and the interpretations that users will place on them. As we shall see, as economic activity grows more complex, real-life instances of single items yielding two or more separate bundles of future economic benefits arise with increasing frequency, and the Statement helps to determine how they should be accounted for.

Control

To qualify as an asset of a given entity, the access to future economic benefits embodied in the item must be controlled by that entity. The Statement of Principles defines *control* thus:

> An entity will control the rights or other access if it has the ability both to obtain for itself any economic benefits that will arise and to prevent or limit the access of others to those benefits. (SP, 4.17)

The most straightforward case arises where: (a) access to future economic benefits is established by legal rights; and (b) the entity controls that access by owning those legal rights. This case generally covers the majority of tangible and monetary assets on most entities' balance sheets: the entity simply owns in law the items of property that give rise to the benefits that qualify as its assets.

In many instances the entity will have a choice as to how it finally obtains the future economic benefits embodied in an asset: it may, for example, own land which it can use in its business, sell, or lease to a third party. All of these alternatives yield benefits for the entity and it controls access to those benefits because it chooses in which form to receive them and can then ensure that they are, indeed, received. A choice is not crucial to the definition, however, so long as there is at least one way in which benefits can be obtained and the entity can ensure that the benefits are delivered to it. Thus, for example, a parcel of land which is subject to planning control and could not be used in the entity's business or leased to a third party can be an asset provided that benefits can be obtained by selling the land.

Control need not be enforceable at law, provided that there are other means, such as economic or social sanctions, that can be used to obtain access. Thus, for example, a refund due to an entity under a guarantee, but not yet paid, can be an asset even if the guarantee is not enforceable at law, provided that the entity has some means of ensuring payment. This might involve, for example, threatening to withdraw its custom from the supplier, where the value of that custom was such that any rational commercial operator would rather pay under the guarantee than lose the business.

No asset can be the asset of more than one entity because two entities cannot control the same rights or other access to a stream of economic benefits. In this context, joint control has no meaning: either an entity can obtain a given stream of benefits for itself alone or it does not control access. As we saw in the previous section, however, a single item can generate more than one stream of benefits and each stream can be controlled by, and thus represent an asset for, a different entity. The example given in the previous section was rather artificial. A more realistic example would be the case of a vehicle purchased by entity A and leased to entity B. In this case entity B controls access to the benefits that come from using the vehicle, perhaps to deliver its output to customers, while A controls access to the stream of rental payments to be made by B under the lease. Hence the same item, the vehicle, generates two streams of economic benefits and thus underpins assets for two entities. The nature of those benefits is different and thus the assets of the two entities are themselves different.

Some entities will have one or a small number of assets that constitute the core of their business as they currently conduct it. Examples here include a hotel operator owning a single hotel and a television station broadcasting under a single franchise: in both cases the asset (the hotel or franchise rights) could not be disposed of without fundamentally altering the character of the entity. The entity nonetheless controls access to the benefits embodied in the asset. It will normally obtain the benefits by continuing to hold the item of property and using it in its business but, if necessary, it could dispose of the item independently of the entity, and acquire the benefits in this way.

The Statement of Principles goes on to point out (SP, 4.21) that some factors which undoubtedly contribute economic benefits to a business, such as market share, superior management or good labour relations, do so in ways that are arguably not under the control of the entity. This is because the entity cannot choose when to obtain those benefits within the business and cannot realize them by sale because they cannot be separated from the business. Hence the benefits can be obtained only by selling the entity as a whole and thus the entity itself does not control them, although its owners may. This point relates to the determination of whether or not goodwill is an asset and we will consider it in more detail later.

Past transactions or events

It is not immediately obvious how this clause in the definition derives from the economic focus of the Statement's approach to assets. It can be read as merely underlining what is implicit in the requirement that, for them to qualify as an asset, access to future economic benefits must be under the control of the entity: to qualify as an asset *at any particular moment in time*, control must already have been established *at that time*. Hence a current expectation of control to be achieved at some time in the future cannot result in an asset at the moment. Since it is difficult to envisage how an entity could come to have control over access to future economic benefits without some transaction or event occurring, the reference to past transactions or events emphasizes (but does not add to) the need for control to have been established by the balance sheet date.

Where operations are undertaken on an orthodox commercial basis, control over goods and services is normally obtained by paying for (or, strictly speaking, agreeing to pay for) the goods or services concerned, and thus a transaction (the acquisition) will have occurred by the balance sheet date and the 'past transaction or event' clause will create no difficulty. Even where profit-seeking entities are operating outside the orthodox commercial basis, as for example when they are offered a government grant towards some operation or purchase, there will usually be *some* transaction or event establishing or confirming entitlement to the future economic benefits involved – perhaps a letter formally confirming the grant, or other events or transactions undertaken by the entity which confirm legal entitlement to a grant under the formal terms of the relevant scheme. Much the same position applies in the case of a third party committing some act against the entity for which a claim for damages arises: there is a past event, namely the original act, which gives rise to the future economic benefits, namely the proceeds from the settlement.

In these instances it is clear that until the transaction or event occurs, the entity does not control access to the future economic benefits. For example, if a grant is sought under a scheme that pays the grant automatically once certain conditions have been satisfied, the entity does not control access to the benefits until all the conditions have been satisfied. If the grant is discretionary, the entity does not control access to the benefits until the awarding body has issued a confirmation of the grant which, for legal or other reasons, it is highly likely to honour. Until the relevant transactions or events have occurred, the awarding body could simply withhold the grant and the entity would have no means of insisting that it was paid: thus it does not control access to the benefits involved.

The explanation of the 'past transactions or events' clause given above corresponds to the gloss put on it by the Statement of Principles itself (SP, 4.22). The reference to past transactions or events chimes with the notion that traditional financial reporting is 'transaction based' and hence objective. This may offer some comfort to those who are suspicious of conceptual frameworks and fear that the Statement of Principles is being used to smuggle in a move to 'future-oriented' methods such as discounted cash flow.

A potential difficulty might arise, however, if a case were to be identified in which an entity clearly had control over access to future economic benefits but there had, at the balance sheet date, been no identifiable transaction or event which could satisfy this clause of the definition. Suppose, for example, that a business in a research-intensive industry, say pharmaceuticals, comes across, as a by-product of work undertaken to develop a particular range of products, a formula for a drug in a field unrelated to the range it was working on. The new drug offers very substantial commercial benefits and the business can control access to these by keeping the formula secret. However, because the formula emerged by chance, there are no transactions or specific events associated with its discovery. The future economic benefits satisfy every other requirement of the definition of assets; they are as secure (and, presumably, as interesting to users of the entity's financial statements) as benefits to be gained from a drug developed deliberately. Yet, it might be argued that they do not qualify as an asset because there is no past transaction or event. It is difficult to justify this position in terms of the Statement of Principles' economic approach and it will be tempting to identify something that can count as an event for the purpose of satisfying the definition – perhaps, in this case, the scientists' realization that the formula would work.

All in all, it can be argued that this clause simply provokes a game of 'hunt the event' rather than representing a significant factor in discriminating between assets and non-assets.

Other aspects of the definition

Uncertainty

All future events are to some degree uncertain: even those which are certain to occur are often uncertain in timing or size. The inescapable uncertainty attaching to all future events is one of the biggest – indeed, perhaps, the biggest – cause of difficulty for accountants. It affects both the existence of assets and their measurement.

It will be helpful as an introduction to this section to examine the impact of uncertainty on orthodox financial reporting. Traditionally, financial reporting has often been thought to have escaped largely or entirely from problems resulting from uncertainty about the future by focusing on past transactions and past (historical) costs. This confidence that financial reporting is unaffected by uncertainty about the future has always been an illusion, not only as far as the underlying rationale for the system is concerned, but also, to at least a limited extent, in terms of the way the system has actually been operated.

It is illuminating to look at some fairly straightforward examples. Stocks have for many years been required to be stated at the lower of cost and net realizable value and the latter will in most instances be a forecast. Thus, although the large majority of stock numbers may in fact be based on cost, these are in effect accompanied by a forecast that net realizable value is in excess of the number stated. Some stocks will actually be stated at (forecast) net realizable value. Debtors have for many years been required to be stated after adjustment for bad and doubtful debts: thus all accounting numbers for debtors are forecasts of what will be collected. Even when the forecast is that there will be no bad and doubtful debts, so that the debtor number equals the ledger balance and legal indebtedness, the figure is used because it is believed to be the amount that will be collected and is thus a forecast. When tangible fixed assets are stated at a carrying amount which reflects cost and accumulated depreciation, the accumulated depreciation (and the depreciation charge in the profit and loss account) will be a function of cost, residual value, economic life and the method employed: two of these are forecasts. If the carrying amount includes a revaluation, all elements in the calculation of the carrying amount other than the depreciation method, itself arguably an arbitrary choice and certainly not one derived from past events, will be forecasts.

The examples cited in the previous paragraph argue that contemporary published financial statements, if they comply properly with current requirements, depend heavily on forecasts. Now, it is possible in practice that statements are drawn up without making many explicit forecasts. For example, it may simply be *assumed* that the cost of stock is below net realizable value (at least until such time as trading conditions deteriorate markedly); equally, in calculating depreciation, residual value may be *assumed* to be immaterial while economic life may be based on standard figures for wide-ranging categories of asset. In these instances, reporting the figures within the framework of GAAP nonetheless implies that, although they may be derived without alteration from past figures or 'rules' (such as standard lives), the figures are acceptable as forecasts.

We can now turn to look at the impact of uncertainty on the Statement of Principles' definition of assets. Uncertainty is, of course, at the core of the definition. No future economic benefits can be certain; nor, even if they eventuate, can it be certain that an entity will be able to control access to them. The uncertainty attaching to future economic benefits is essentially the same as the uncertainty to be reflected in the forecasts required by traditional financial statements. In the main, uncertainty affects the measurement of assets rather than their existence (a matter to which we turn in Chapter 8), but in some cases there will be uncertainty as to whether an individual asset exists at all. Thus a debtor may become insolvent and fail to pay: this will mean the future economic benefits to be derived from the settlement of the debt will not eventuate and the debtor will not be an asset. This is simply another way of looking at the need to adjust debtors for bad and doubtful debts under the traditional approach to financial reporting. Equally, a physical resource may be destroyed in a fire or other catastrophe and, if uninsured for that particular risk, will yield no economic benefits to the entity. In the (admittedly rare) event that this is thought at the balance sheet date to be highly likely, there is no asset: equally, under traditional financial reporting there should be an impairment adjustment to bring the carrying amount down to nil.

The definition in the Statement of Principles does not refer explicitly to the uncertainty attaching to future economic benefits and in this respect is unlike the US conceptual framework which defines assets in terms of 'probable future economic benefits' (SFAC 6, paragraph 25, emphasis added). However, the US Statement goes on to indicate that the term 'probable' is used in a general sense and not with any technical meaning, so that it is not to be read, for example, as requiring a probability of occurrence in excess of 0.5.

The presence or absence of an explicit reference to uncertainty does not really alter the character of an asset under the definition. It is inherent in the nature of the world that financial reporting seeks to capture that assets are derived from future events about which there is inescapable uncertainty, and it is impossible to provide a definition of assets that enables accountants to escape the judgements and forecasts necessitated by that uncertainty. A definition of assets that required future benefits to be certain would eradicate assets from the financial statements of 'real-world' entities. The nature of the uncertainty that surrounds most business transactions means that it is not possible to apply a definition in terms of a technical test for the degree of certainty – that is, it is not possible to say that the probability that economic benefits will eventuate should be in excess of 0.5, or 0.8, or whatever. The definition of assets thus simply accepts that there will be uncertainty; however, the degree of uncertainty surrounding a given bundle of future economic benefits will affect whether and how the relevant asset is recognized in the financial statements (see Chapter 7).

The existence of uncertainty will mean that, as time passes after a given balance sheet date and hindsight can be brought to bear on the situation, items included in the balance sheet as assets may turn out not to qualify under the definition – because the economic benefits have not materialized, or have not been enjoyed by the entity. Equally, other items, not included in the balance sheet, may in fact yield economic benefits to which the entity controls access – so that they did in fact qualify under the definition. It is worth repeating that this could (and does) occur under the model of accounting currently employed and is not a problem introduced into the financial reporting world by the

Statement's definitions. The way in which these occurrences are reported under the Statement of Principles is dealt with in Chapter 7.

The Statement of Principles (SP, 4.16) points out that, because there does not have to be certainty that economic benefits will eventuate, an item can qualify as an asset even if prices at the balance sheet date mean that there would be no benefit at those prices. Consider the case of an option to acquire a parcel of shares in three months' time, at £2 per share. The option is held by an entity at its balance sheet date. Suppose that the price of those shares at the balance sheet date is £1.50: if the option had to be exercised at the balance sheet date it would not in fact be exercised because it would be cheaper to buy shares on the open market (at £1.50) than to exercise the option (at £2). If the entity expects the market price of the shares to rise to £2.50 by the actual exercise date for the option, that option gives rise to an asset for the entity because the entity expects to buy shares for £2 which it can then sell for £2.50.

Cost

Although accountants are used to dealing with assets in terms of their cost, there is nothing in the Statement's definition that requires that assets should have a known cost, or even, indeed, a cost at all. An entity may have access to future economic benefits (which also satisfy the other requirements of the definition) as a result of past transactions, without necessarily knowing which particular past transactions gave rise to the prospect of future benefits. For example, the entity may have run a series of advertisements and now expect future sales as a result of the adver-tisements without being able to specify which particular advertisements in the series were successful. As a consequence, it will not know the cost of obtaining the future benefits. Commercial organizations are occa-sionally given access to future benefits (for example a government grant or a right to operate denied to others) free of charge, and such access can thus represent an asset without an associated cost. Not-for-profit entities may obtain a substantial proportion of their assets without cost. Satis-fying the definition of an asset is only one of several hurdles to inclusion in the balance sheet: while the lack of a known cost does not preclude access to future economic benefits from satisfying the definition of an asset, it may cause difficulties in relation to these other hurdles (see Chapters 7 and 8).

Comprehensiveness

The Statement of Principles' system of element definitions is compre-hensive, in that no items failing to satisfy the definition of one of the elements can be included in the financial statements. Further, only one element, namely assets, can be included in the balance sheet as a resource of the entity. It follows from this that no debit entry in the entity's underlying records can be included in the balance sheet of the entity unless either (a) it satisfies the definition of an asset, or (b) it represents a 'negative' subdivision of ownership interest, that is one resulting from an excess of liabilities over assets.

Valuation accounts

The mechanics of GAAP frequently give rise to amounts by which assets are adjusted. Examples here include accumulated depreciation on tangible fixed assets, provisions for bad debts and provisions for reduction in the carrying amount of stock to net realizable value. However they are treated in the financial statements, valuation accounts are conceptually adjustments to the carrying amount of the asset rather than separate elements in themselves. Thus, for example, accumulated depreciation does not, as we shall see, satisfy the definition of a liability (see Chapter 5). Because the system of definitions is comprehensive, it follows that accumulated depreciation does not qualify for inclusion in the balance sheet as a separate carrying amount. Rather, it represents an adjustment to the carrying amount of an asset, namely the item on which depreciation is being charged.

Criticisms of the definition

As we have seen, the Statement of Principles' element definitions are at the heart of its conceptual framework and the definition of assets is at the heart of the system of definitions. Some commentators reject the whole system, mainly because of the items it would prevent from satisfying the definitions of assets and liabilities, and thus propel into gains and losses. We will examine this criticism later, once the full system has been unveiled. In this section, we look at some rather narrower criticisms.

In the main, the system's focus on an economic, rather than a legal, world view has met widespread support. It is, however, worth noting at this stage that by accepting that all future economic benefits qualify as assets, without examining the nature or degree of uncertainty attaching to them, the *definition* of assets does nothing to address the important problems that result from this uncertainty, thereby simply postponing the need to address these to later stages in the project. The ambiguity surrounding the 'past transactions or events' clause is also a potential source of difficulty, as discussed above.

The way in which the definition is set out obscures a potentially quite serious problem in its operationalization. The definition is written to apply to assets in the plural and refers to economic benefits in the plural.

An asset (in the singular) will be underpinned by a bundle of economic benefits (in the plural); it may correspond to a single item or it may not, as when a single item yields two or more bundles of economic benefits underpinning separate assets for separate entities. We are left to decide, independently of the definition, how to divide up all the economic benefits in the world into bundles for the purposes of applying the definition. Even if we were to attempt to start with individual items, we would rapidly encounter problems because the external world which financial reporting attempts to capture does not in fact divide in a natural and self-evident way into separate individual items.

To take a fairly simple example, consider a fleet of articulated lorries. Is it the fleet (which might well have been bought in a single transaction) that constitutes the item? Is each lorry a separate item? Can the cabs and the trailers (which can probably be bought separately) count as separate items? If we count a cab and its trailer as separate items because they were purchased separately, should we count the set of tyres which were bought separately from the vehicle as an item (or several items)? Where should we stop in the process of disaggregation? It would seem inappropriate to take the way we happen actually to purchase items as constituting the level at which to apply the test because this may mean that whether a particular bundle of benefits yields an asset will depend on a, possibly arbitrary, decision about how items were procured.

It is clear from the discussion in the Statement of Principles that it is envisaged that many assets will reflect the sorts of items that are found in conventional balance sheets (see, for example, paragraph 4.15 which discusses cash, debtors, investments and prepayments). Because accountants are used to dealing with items like this, and habitually divide them up in conventional ways for the purpose of processing the relevant transactions, it is easy to fall into a habit of thinking that presupposes that the conventional ways we use to purchase resources and process transactions somehow arise in nature, but they do not. There is nothing about the fleet of lorries described in the previous paragraph, for example, that tells us what constitutes a separate item or a separate bundle of economic benefits.

And this could have serious consequences for the balance sheet. Consider, for example, a business that needs a warehouse to store its raw materials. The only conveniently located warehouse has ten identical bays and, although the business only requires eight bays at its current level of operations (which it does not expect to increase in the foreseeable future), it is cheaper to buy the warehouse and leave two bays empty than to use other accommodation located further away. If we apply the definition of assets at the level of the warehouse, the warehouse is an asset. If we apply the definition at the level of each bay, eight are assets and two are not. In a cost-based balance sheet, the resulting carrying amount for storage capacity could differ by 20%, depending on whether aggregate cost or cost per bay is used.[4]

The Statement of Principles does not define the term 'future economic benefits'. Some commentators have argued that its coverage of what the phrase implies, and, in particular, the role of cash in this discussion, is confused. The Statement explains that, 'future economic benefits eventually result in net cash inflows to the entity' (SP, 4.15). However, cash itself is an asset, not because it will result in future cash inflows but because it can be spent. Further confusion is caused because as we have seen: (a) cash may not represent an asset (as when it is in a 'blocked' foreign currency; and (b) something may be an asset when no cash inflow will result from it, as in the case of the oil company which pays its dividends in barrels of oil.

The first step in removing this confusion is to look at the Statement of Principles' explanation of the reason that cash itself is an asset: 'the command that cash gives over resources is the basis of its future economic benefits' (SP, 4.15(a)). Other assets also give command over resources: in the large majority of cases, this involves obtaining cash first so that it can then be exchanged for resources, but this stage is not strictly necessary and a direct exchange still results in realization of a command over resources; equally if cash cannot be exchanged for resources it is not an asset.

So can we say that the future economic benefits are the future resources over which the entity will have command? There would be a strong element of circularity here because the items satisfying the definition of assets are themselves economic resources, so that the system would come close to saying that:

1   Assets are future economic resources.
2   Future economic resources are current economic resources (because they can be exchanged in future for other economic resources).
3   Current economic resources are assets.

We would be left seeking to define current economic resources – and we could not do so by saying that they were future economic resources, any more than we could satisfactorily define a dog as something that will tomorrow satisfy the definition of a dog.

This circularity can be avoided by characterizing future economic benefits in terms of the potential for individuals to consume goods and services and thereby obtain enjoyment. Thus, however long the chain of exchanges of one sort of resource for another, and regardless of whether cash appears in this chain, what ultimately underpins an asset is the potential for ending the chain and using the resources to make a distribution to the owners of the entity which they can use for consumption – for *their* benefit. This enables us to escape from the circularity but does further underline the role of investors in the model.

Applications of the definition

In this section we look at how the definition of assets in the Statement of Principles works when applied to a range of different items. Some of these applications are straightforward and the application serves to illustrate the concepts underlying the definition; in other cases the circumstances are more complex and the application of the definition helps to resolve the question of whether, and under what circumstances, the business has an asset.

In our discussions, we will need to take some care with terminology. We will need to distinguish between the actual 'things' to be tested (debtors, lorries, and so on) and the streams of future economic benefits those 'things' can embody. Equally, we will need to distinguish between those streams of future economic benefits which satisfy the definition of assets and those that do not. The Statement of Principles uses the term *item* or *item of property* for the things themselves. We should, strictly speaking, avoid using the term 'asset' to describe any item of property, though it is sometimes difficult to do so in practice. It follows that we need to avoid using the term 'asset' in describing classes of items not yet tested, because this begs the question. Thus, for example, we need to avoid referring to brands in general as intangible assets because this begs the question as to whether some or all would fail to satisfy the definition of assets. Equally, we should use the phrase 'current assets' to refer not to cash, debtors and stock in general but only to those items of cash, debtors and stock that satisfy the definition of assets. Finally we need to distinguish between items that satisfy the Statement of Principles' definition of assets and items that are permitted under GAAP to be treated as assets but which may or may not satisfy the Statement of Principles' definition (we will refer to the latter as *GAAP assets*).

Cash

As we have seen, the future economic benefits to be derived from cash in hand and at bank will almost invariably qualify as assets. The future economic benefits will come from the use of the cash to purchase other resources (to be used to generate benefits), to settle debts (which would otherwise need to be settled by sacrificing other resources, so that the benefit from owning the cash comes from not having to sacrifice the other resources), or to make a distribution to owners (when the benefit comes from being able to make a valuable transfer to owners without having to sacrifice other resources).

Control over access to the benefits comes, in the case of cash in hand, from legal ownership and physical custody, and, in the case of cash at bank, from legal rights over the bank balance. In the case of cash at bank, the 'past transaction or event' will generally be depositing the amount with the bank, as evidenced by a bank statement or certificate. In the case of cash in hand, it will be the physical receipt of the cash, generally evidenced by the continued physical presence of the cash at the balance sheet date.

In rare cases cash may not qualify as an asset because the entity does not control access to the future economic benefits to be obtained from deploying it. One example would be cash at bank held in a foreign territory under a regime which offered little or no realistic prospect of the entity being able to use the balance for its benefit within the territory or withdraw it from the country concerned. Another might be cash physically held by the entity as a result of fraudulent transactions, where the recovery of the cash by the rightful owner was virtually assured.

Stock

The future economic benefits to be derived from stock will usually qualify as an asset. Stock is normally owned by the purchasing entity as soon as it is delivered and in this way the entity will control access to the future economic benefits embodied in it. These benefits will come about in different ways according to the type of stock:

1   Finished goods will be sold and generate cash, which we have already seen will usually give rise to an asset.
2   Work in progress will be converted into finished goods, which will generate benefits as outlined in 1.
3   Raw materials will be converted into work in progress, which generates benefits as outlined in 2.
4   Goods purchased for resale generate cash, as in 1.
5   Consumables (fuel, lubricants, stationery and so on) are used up in the manufacture of finished goods or in delivering services and generate benefits in the same way as raw materials, as outlined in 3.

Stock presents an interesting example of the game of 'hunt the event' referred to earlier. Clearly for stocks of raw materials, goods for resale and consumables the event is the purchase transaction and can be evidenced by a goods received note. According to Weetman, the past transaction or event for work in progress is 'evaluation of the state of completion of the work, evidenced by work records', while for finished goods it is 'transfer from production line to finished goods store, evidenced by internal transfer form' (1999: 31). But there are problems here. We might begin by asking whether 'evaluation of the state of completion of the work' qualifies as a transaction or an event for the purposes of satisfying the definition. Clearly, management or auditors inspecting the stock *is* an event, but it is not an event that *results in* control, which either exists before the inspection or not at all. If we treat this sort of event as satisfying the definition, no item will ever fail the definition as a result of this clause because it will always be possible to say of any item that someone has checked it, using whatever method is appropriate to items of that class. However deficient the method, or indeed its application in any particular case, the check will constitute an event. Hence, the clause would have no power at all to discriminate between items that could give rise to assets and items that do not, and would thus be redundant. What we need is a transaction or event that gives control over access to benefits.

The entity does not control access to the future economic benefits embodied in work in progress or finished goods solely because it has carried out the conversion work, as can be demonstrated by considering a case where a manufacturing jeweller creates a piece from gold and diamonds supplied by the customer. In this case the future economic benefits embodied in the piece probably belong to the customer already, subject to payment for the jeweller's labour. Hence, in the normal case, the future economic benefits are controlled by the entity because it has legal and constructive ownership of the stock. In order to demonstrate securely that it has legal and constructive ownership of the stock, an entity may have to show that: (a) it owned the raw materials, consumables and other items used up in its manufacture; (b) it paid or will pay for the services used up in its manufacture; (c) it supplied the infrastructure within which the stock was manufactured; and (d) it initiated and managed the conversion process. Conceptually, all these can be traced back to past transactions or events and thus stock, in the abstract, can give rise to assets. In the case of any particular item of stock, however, tracing the complex web of transactions and events that give rise to ownership would be very difficult. This demonstrates, not that stock cannot give rise to an asset, but that the existence of the 'past transaction or event' clause in the definition is probably redundant: what counts is that the entity owns the stock and thus controls access to its benefits.

It is reasonably common for suppliers dealing with other businesses to include in the contract of sale a 'reservation of title' clause. Under this clause, the seller retains legal title to the goods supplied until the customer pays for them. The main purpose of this clause is to give an unpaid seller a better claim if the purchaser becomes insolvent: whether such a clause is effective in any particular case depends on the construction of the contract in that case. Does an effective reservation of title clause mean that stock delivered but not paid for is not an asset of the purchaser because it does not have legal ownership of the stock? Under GAAP, the stock is normally treated as an asset of the purchaser, especially where the purchaser is a going concern such that there is little likelihood that the reservation will be exercised. This is consistent with the definition in the Statement of Principles because the entity effectively controls access to the future economic benefits once it has taken custody of the stock: in order to receive those benefits it will also have to pay for the stock in due course, but that might well also be true of stock purchased without a reservation of title clause in that, if the entity does not pay its bills, it may not survive long enough to enjoy the benefits from that stock.

It is true that, at least in the case of stock sold subject to reservation of title, in order to continue to control access to benefits, the entity must undertake *future* events, such as paying for the stock in due time, in addition to the *past* event (taking delivery) which has given control over access to those benefits. This is, however, the case for most assets: for example, in the case of a vehicle bought and paid for, if the entity is going actually to be able to obtain benefits from that vehicle by using it to deliver goods, it will have to undertake a series of future events including insuring it, maintaining it, garaging it, and so on.

As with cash, we should not fall into the habit of thinking that, because stock is almost invariably an asset, it will always be so. Stocks of finished goods which the entity will not now be able to sell at all (perhaps because of changed legislation or a health scare) are not assets because there are no future economic benefits embodied in them. If the entity can sell the stocks, but at a price below cost, they remain eligible to qualify as assets (because there are future benefits) but the issue of how they should be measured may arise (see Chapter 8).

Debtors

Debtors will generally give rise to assets: the future economic benefits are the cash to be received when the debtor pays; the past transaction or event will usually be the delivery of the stock in accordance with an explicit or implicit contract of sale which involves subsequent payment; and control over access to the benefit flows from the contract, perhaps with possession of sufficient evidence to enforce the contract (such as a signed receipt for the goods). A debtor may fail the definition if it is unlikely that it will in fact pay the debt (no future economic benefits) or the evidence to enforce the contract is lost (no control).

Prepayments

Prepayments are payments for goods and services made in advance of delivery. Prepayment may be required for goods to be manufactured to a customer's specification or for a range of services including, for example, insurance. Prepayment generally establishes for the entity making the payment a legal or constructive right to delivery of the goods or services involved and thus gives the entity control over access to the future economic benefits embodied in the goods or services. The past transaction or event is the act of making the payment. Hence, prepayments will generally qualify as assets.[5]

Fixed tangibles

Fixed tangibles, such as land, buildings, plant, machinery, fixtures and fittings, tools, equipment and vehicles, will normally generate future economic benefits, usually either (a) as they are used by the entity in the course of producing its output (thus enabling that output to be sold for cash and avoiding the need to expend further cash to obtain the production capacity available from the tangibles under consideration), or (b) by being sold. Where the entity owns the tangibles it will generally have a legal right to control access to those future economic benefits: the past transaction or event will be the transaction by which it acquired ownership. Hence the item will qualify as an asset.

Because they are often large and 'lumpy', fixed tangibles can give rise to practical problems which, as discussed earlier, are, in conceptual terms, equivalent to asking 'Is this one asset or several?' Such problems can arise, for example, in deciding how to treat a fleet of vehicles or a building which has had several extensions added to it at various times. One specific case of this type, oil wells, is dealt with later in this section; and another, unusable capacity, has already been examined.

Leased items

In straightforward cases a lease is a contract under which one party (the lessor), which has legal ownership of a resource such as a building or a vehicle, permits another party (the lessee) to use that resource over an extended period in return for a stream of payments. The term of a lease is often roughly equal to the expected economic life of the resource and in this case the contract is sometimes referred to as a *full pay-out lease*.

Let us begin by considering the case of a full pay-out lease for, say, an aircraft, from the perspective of the lessee, an airline. The future economic benefits embodied in the aircraft will materialize as it is used to transport passengers and those benefits will be received by the airline in the form of fares. The contract enables the airline to use the aircraft in its business, to prevent others from using it, and to prevent the lessor from recovering possession provided that the airline makes the necessary payments under the lease. Hence, it controls access to the future economic benefits and they can qualify as an asset. The balance sheet of the airline will also include a corresponding liability for the payments to be made under the lease.

Now let us consider a case where the term is substantially shorter than the full pay-out period, say 50% of that period. Under the definitions in the Statement of Principles, nothing changes. The future economic benefits embodied in the use of the aircraft for the first half of its operating life represent an asset and it is the asset of the airline because the airline controls access to those benefits by enforcing the terms of the lease. The remaining benefits will accrue to some other party (the lessor, unless another lease has already been written). We have already seen that the same item of property can underpin two or more assets for different parties.

Finally, the lessor also has an asset resulting from the lease but the lessor's asset flows from the stream of rental payments to be made by the lessee (in other words, it is the debtor balance that corresponds to the lessee's liability). These future economic benefits will normally take the form of cash receipts (though they may be realized by repossessing the aircraft if the payments are not made) and access to them is controlled by the lessor as a result of its rights under the lease.

The traditional method of accounting for leases in practice derived from the ownership model of assets. The lessee did not *own* the property which was the subject of the lease and hence did not include an asset in its balance sheet; equally, the stream of payments due to the lessor were excluded from the balance sheet. This approach came to be regarded as unsatisfactory by users of financial statements, not as a result of their concern for conceptual rigour but rather because investors in failing companies discovered that those companies had very substantial and legally enforceable commitments to make payments to lessors which were not showing as liabilities on the entities' balance sheets (see Davies et al., 1999: 1161).

As a result of these concerns, GAAP was altered to require leases that transferred 'substantially all the risks and rewards of ownership of an asset to the lessee' (SSAP21, paragraph 15) to be accounted for by the recognition of an asset and a liability in the way outlined above. SSAP21 described such leases as *finance leases*. Although the wording is slightly different, we can think of finance leases as those for which access to substantially all the future economic benefits is controlled by the lessee. Thus GAAP, in the form of SSAP21, is consistent with the Statement of Principles' definition of an asset in the case of finance leases.

Leases which do not satisfy the definition of finance leases are referred to as *operating leases* under SSAP21. Some of these will genuinely be short-term rental agreements, that is, the lease is either written to last only for a short period, or can be cancelled by either party at short notice and without penalty. Under such leases, the future economic benefits to which the lessee controls access will have more or less expired by the date of the next balance sheet. However SSAP21's operating leases also include leases which involve a significant proportion of the economic benefits embodied in the item (but less than 'substantially all' of them). The latter category satisfies the Statement of Principles' definition of an asset for the lessee but, under SSAP21, they are not GAAP assets. The period's rental payment is charged in the profit and loss account but nothing appears in the balance sheet, although there may be substantial future economic benefits embodied in the lease to which the lessee controls access and, equally, the lessee may be committed to a substantial stream of future payments. Even the former category – short-term rental agreements – falls within the definition of assets at the time the lease is written.

Entities may have an incentive to classify leases as operating leases to keep the asset and associated liability off the balance sheet. One method of manoeuvring leases into the operating category is to set the proportion of risks and rewards just below the level that would count as 'substantially all', so that leases for which access to *most* of the economic benefits is under the control of the lessee are nonetheless classified as operating leases. Another method involves writing into the lease one or more 'break clauses', that is options for the lessee to cancel the lease. Under SSAP21, where it is 'reasonably certain at the inception of the lease' (paragraph 19) that the lease will be extended, for example because the penalty for cancellation is so large that it is not commercially viable for the entity to exercise this option, the calculation of the proportion of economic benefits transferred must assume that the lease is extended. However, the parties may agree a break clause which is expensive to exercise and, on balance, unlikely to be exercised but which is not so punitive as to make it *reasonably certain* that it will not be exercised, and this will make the lease eligible for treatment as an operating lease.

Under either of the sets of circumstances outlined above, two agreements which are very similar in their commercial effect can be shown in very different ways in the financial statements. Taking the first example, one lease may shift just one or two percentage points more of the future economic benefits to the lessee than the other but the first will then appear on the balance sheet while the second does not.

A study by the G4+1 Group (McGregor, 1996) examined the problems caused by current GAAP in a number of countries, including the UK, and recommended a new approach. It pointed out that most, if not all, leases, other than those genuinely cancellable by both parties without penalty and at very short notice, give rise to streams of future economic benefits for the lessee which satisfy the definition of assets in the Statement of Principles (and those in other conceptual frameworks used in the G4+1 regimes). As a result it recommended that G4+1 standard-setters should consider revising standards so that non-cancellable leases would be recognized as assets and liabilities, subject to the application of the criteria and measurement methods specified in the relevant conceptual framework.

One argument in favour of the new approach is that it solves some of the problems associated with current GAAP, including: (a) the treatment of similar transactions in markedly dissimilar ways, according to minor characteristics such as the exact percentage of future economic benefits transferred under the lease; and (b) the artificial construction of transactions as a response to the way the accounting standard is written. However, the more significant argument is that it should (if the arguments in the Statement of Principles are correct) provide more useful information about the resources, obligations and future cash flows of the entity. This is because significant future economic benefits under the control of the entity, and significant obligations to transfer benefits, are reported to users on the new approach but omitted from the financial statements under the old approach.

This argument is keyed to the overall objective of financial reporting and demonstrates how the new approach takes us nearer to satisfying that objective. It is thus more persuasive than one that simply says, pragmatically, 'Here is a problem with current GAAP and here is a new method that doesn't have that particular problem.' The difficulty with the latter approach is that the new method may have other problems that are worse than the one being cured. This new approach to accounting for leases thus represents an illustration of the argument that conceptual frameworks can provide better guidance to standard-setters and move GAAP towards better quality financial reporting rather than merely fire-fighting.[6]

Securities

This section deals with securities held as 'simple investments' (FRS9), that is, we are excluding cases where the entity holding the securities itself exercises or shares control over the entity whose securities are held (see Chapter 10) and the holding by an entity of its own securities.

Most securities offer the owners the prospect of a stream of future income in the form of near-certain interest (debt instruments) or relatively risky dividends (equity instruments), together with the opportunity to liquidate the capital invested in the holding, either by selling the security on to a third party or by repayment from the issuing entity. Under normal circumstances, the future income stream and opportunity to liquidate the investment will represent future economic benefits, the investing entity will control access to those benefits by virtue of owning the securities, and the purchase of the securities will represent a past transaction: thus the securities will satisfy the definition of an asset.

As in other cases, a particular investment in securities may not satisfy the definition of an asset if, for example, there is no prospect of receiving future income (or cash from liquidating the investment), say if a speculative mining company has failed to find the minerals for which it was prospecting; or if the investing entity does not control access to future benefits, perhaps because the underlying operations which will generate returns are located in a foreign regime which is now politically unstable or where there is a high probability that the operations will be nationalized without compensation.

Oil and gas exploration and production

Prospecting for hydrocarbon deposits, especially offshore and in hostile onshore locations such as deserts, is an extremely expensive business. Typically, companies will first obtain seismic data and geological analyses for an area (known as a 'field'), then: (a) purchase licences to explore parts of the field, usually from the relevant government and at significant cost; (b) conduct further and more expensive surveys; and (c) drill 'exploration wells' to establish physically whether there are deposits in the area and, if so, their size. Where commercially viable deposits are found, further 'development wells' will be drilled and the infrastructure needed to exploit the field will be constructed. Total expenditure on a single field may run to many hundreds of millions of pounds.

It is easy to see that a commercially viable field yields streams of future economic benefits (in the form of oil and gas which can be sold), that access to these benefits will usually be under the control of the prospecting entity (legally, because it holds the licence for the field, and substantively, because it owns the wells and infrastructure needed to bring the oil and gas to the surface), and that this control flows from past transactions and events (purchase of the licence, prospecting activity, and so on).

Current GAAP (OIAC SORP2) permits two quite different approaches to the treatment of oil and gas exploration costs. Under the first, the *successful efforts* method, all costs of exploring the field as a whole and all costs of drilling wells which do not result in the discovery and development of commercially viable reserves are expensed as incurred (that is, not capitalized, or, using the language of the Statement of Principles, not recognized as an asset). Only costs relating directly to the discovery and development of commercially viable reserves are capitalized (recognized as assets). Each well is assessed individually as having been successful or not, and only successful wells are capitalized.

The alternative approach is the *full cost* method. All costs of exploring and developing a particular geographical area are capitalized. The area is specified by the entity in relation to its own activities, and might be a field, a licence area within a field, or even the whole world. The capitalized cost is then depreciated against the revenue stream from the area, which will, obviously, come from the successful wells.

Clearly the amount of expenditure capitalized (and thus the pattern of revenue flows after write-offs and depreciation) may differ very substantially between the two methods. The rationale for the successful efforts method is that unsuccessful ('dry') wells yield no future economic benefits and thus cannot qualify as assets. The rationale for the full cost method is that there is no way of knowing *in advance* which wells will be successful, so that, realistically, the cost of finding the oil and gas that is found includes the efforts that turn out to be unsuccessful, as well as the costs of exploring the field as a whole for potential drilling sites. In traditional terms, the successful efforts method can be defended as *prudent* while full cost can be defended as better *matching* the overall cost of finding the oil and gas in a field against the revenue earned from it (SSAP2, paragraph 14).

The crucial issue from the point of view of the Statement of Principles is the identity of the item in which are embodied the future economic benefits which will flow from the exploitation of the field. Does the definition of assets help in indicating which is the better method? Unfortunately, it does not appear to. What we need is guidance on the level of aggregation at which we are to apply the test of whether an item qualifies as an asset. Once we have this, the solution will be simple: if we are to apply it at the level of the field, the full cost method is appropriate, while if we are to look to individual wells, the successful efforts method should be required. Unfortunately the definition does not offer any insight into this particular issue. This is not to suggest that the Statement of Principles cannot help in resolving the problem: what will be needed, however, is an examination of the usefulness of the two alternative methods in terms of the objective of financial reporting, rather than merely the routine application of the definition of assets.

Research and development

In many industries, businesses need to undertake substantial levels of research and development activity in pursuit of new products and processes: without this level of activity, a business will not survive because its existing range of products and services will become obsolete and it will have nothing to replace it with. Well-known examples include the pharmaceuticals, electronics and defence industries.

According to SSAP13, research and development embraces three categories:

(a)   Pure (or basic) research: experimental or theoretical work undertaken primarily to acquire new scientific or technical knowledge for its own sake rather than directed towards any specific aim or application.

(b)   Applied research: original or critical investigation undertaken in order to gain new scientific or technical knowledge and directed towards a specific practical aim or objective.

(c)   Development: use of scientific or technical knowledge in order to produce new or substantially improved materials, devices, products or services, to install new processes or systems prior to the commencement of commercial production or commercial applications, or to improve substantially those already produced or installed. (paragraph 21)

The motivation for any profit-seeking entity to undertake research and development, even the purest of research, is ultimately to generate future economic benefits, in the form of revenue from the products and services that emerge from the process. In determining whether this research and development can satisfy the definition of an asset, the issues under the approach of the Statement of Principles are: (a) whether, at any given moment, past activity (and thus cost) can be associated with future economic benefits; (b) whether access to any stream of future economic benefits can be identified as controlled by the entity; and (c) whether appropriate past transactions and events can be identified.

Taking development activity (as defined above) first, it is quite likely that, for specific projects that are commercially viable, it will be possible to identify a stream of future economic benefits and past transactions and events associated with the project, and that access to the benefits will be controlled by the entity, for example because it owns a patent or can prevent others from acquiring the know-how needed to exploit the discovery. Hence it may well be that development expenditure will satisfy the definition of an asset.

In the case of applied research, it is less likely that activity will satisfy the definition, either because, though there is a 'specific practical aim or objective' (SSAP13, paragraph 21(b)), there is no specific project that could yield future economic benefits; or because, although there is such a project, it is too early in its life to establish that there will be future economic benefits. An example of the first case would be applied research to find practical uses for a new chemical that had emerged from pure research experimentation. Nonetheless, it does seem possible that occasionally a piece of applied research could have future economic benefits associated with it sufficiently closely to mean that it could satisfy the definition of an asset. In the case of pure research, the likelihood of it being possible to identify a stream of future economic benefits that could satisfy the definition of an asset is perhaps very remote – though, since the definition of pure research is given in terms of intention, whereas that of an asset is given in terms of outcome, it still seems possible.

Current GAAP (SSAP13) is that, where development expenditure satisfies certain tests, there is a free choice as to whether it is treated as a GAAP asset or expensed immediately. Pure and applied research, and development activity that does not pass the tests, must not be treated as a GAAP asset. The tests to be applied to development expenditure before it can be capitalized are as follows:

(a) there is a clearly defined project, and
(b) the related expenditure is separately identifiable, and
(c) the outcome of such a project has been assessed with reasonable certainty as to:
  (i)   its technical feasibility, and
  (ii) its ultimate commercial viability considered in the light of factors such as likely market conditions (including completed products), public opinion, consumer and environmental legislation, and
(d) the aggregate of the deferred development costs, any further development costs, and related production, selling and administrative costs is reasonably expected to be exceeded by related future sales or other revenues, and

(e)   adequate resources exist, or are reasonably expected to be available, to enable the project to be completed and to provide any consequential increase in working capital. (paragraph 25)

Although the standard was adopted well before work on the Statement of Principles began, the tests can be seen as an attempt to establish that development expenditure qualified as an asset, in other words to implement a definition of the term 'asset'. Clauses (c), (d) and (e) address questions which come close to what we can now talk about in terms of there being future economic benefits (clauses (c) and (d)), access to which are controlled by the entity because it will be able to complete the project and thereby exploit the development expenditure (clause (e)).[7]

Overall, then, the approach of current GAAP can be regarded as one way of coming reasonably close to an implementation of the definition of assets in the Statement of Principles. Research will rarely satisfy the definition and cannot be recognized as a GAAP asset. Development expenditure may, under certain circumstances, satisfy the definition and may be recognized as a GAAP asset, subject to tests which approximate to the definition (and recognition criteria) of the Statement. Although free choices of accounting policy are generally regarded as undesirable, the ASB has eliminated some and it may be hoped that this one too will be eliminated sooner or later.

In determining whether or not development expenditure can be capitalized, it is clear from what has been said above that the basic item to be examined is the individual project. Individual projects that will not yield future economic benefits are not assets. This approach can be contrasted with oil and gas exploration, where the full costing method implies that the item is the geographical area or field rather than the individual well. In order to discover a particular, commercially viable, field, it is necessary to prospect the field and drill several wells, some of which will be dry. In order to discover a particular drug, it may be necessary to undertake applied research across a field of activity and, perhaps, to seek to develop several unsuccessful projects alongside the successful one.

Yet in one case the item to be tested is the field and unsuccessful efforts are viewed as part of the cost of the field, while in the other the item is the individual project and unsuccessful efforts, considered separately, fail to satisfy the definition of an asset. This demonstrates that, in meeting the objective of financial statements, application of the definitions is a starting point rather than a mechanical exercise.

Intangibles

For the purposes of this discussion, we can think of intangibles as non-financial, non-physical items which can be identified separately from the business as a whole and which may be able to be exploited by the entity to achieve future economic benefits. This definition excludes *goodwill* which is associated with the business as a whole but cannot be attributed to separately identifiable items and factors: goodwill is dealt with later in this section.

In part because intangibles lack physical or financial form, it is difficult to say with any precision what should and what should not count as an intangible. For example, it will frequently be the case that businesses will expect to earn higher returns than they otherwise might because they have a well-established portfolio of clients who are likely to return to them with further commissions or a loyal and expert workforce who are likely to continue in their employment. Do these factors amount to intangibles? In the normal case the answer is likely to be 'no' because, although it is possible to name the factors, and perhaps to demonstrate that they exist in any particular case, it will not be possible to establish the effect of any one factor with sufficient confidence to say that it has been identified separately from the business as a whole. Thus to list the factors is really to explain the causes of goodwill rather than to identify a separate intangible. However, in principle, it is possible that there might be cases in which the effect of a portfolio of clients or a loyal workforce could be identified separately with sufficient confidence to constitute an intangible.

Some items have rather greater potential for separate identification than those discussed in the previous paragraph. A number of developments in the business world have greatly increased the role of intangibles in recent years. These developments include:

1   the enormous expansion in knowledge-based industries, which give rise to intangibles such as patents and know-how
2   the increasing profile of marketing, which gives rise to intangibles such as brands, trademarks, mailing lists and mastheads
3   the emergence of business 'networks', which give rise to intangibles such as franchises
4   privatization accompanied by the creation of regulatory authorities, which give rise to intangibles such as quotas, licences, permits and landing rights.

All the items listed above can yield future economic benefits for an entity, for example by enabling its products to be sold at higher prices (brands), or enabling the product to be delivered at all (patents, franchises, landing rights or a licence to broadcast). In some cases, it may be clear that access to these future economic benefits is controlled by the entity. Many intangibles involve legal rights (patents, trademarks, franchises, licences, permits, and so on) and if a third party attempts to exploit the intangible, say by manufacturing a patented product, using a trademark on its own goods, or broadcasting on a wavelength or in an area for which another broadcaster holds the licence, legal steps can be taken to prevent the abuse and recover any profits made by the third party.

In other cases, the entity may have physical custody of the information or other resource needed to exploit the intangible: for example it may be able to keep know-how secret or treat a mailing list as confidential. This sort of arrangement may be less effective than legal rights and there may be situations in which an entity may be attempting to maintain secrecy but with only a limited likelihood that it will succeed: for example it may be difficult to retain control over a mailing list in a computerized environment with high staff turnover, so unless this is backed up by some prospect of preventing competitors from using the information if it is made available to them, there may be little assurance that the entity does control access to the relevant benefits. In some cases, control over access to benefits is underpinned by rights over some item that is associated with the intangible: for example control over access to the benefits expected to flow from a brand may be achieved by legal rights over the trademarks which are used to promote the brand.

Finally, of course, there needs to be a past transaction or event. In many cases there clearly will be: a trademark will have been registered or purchased, a franchise or licence will have been granted or purchased. In other cases it may be possible to identify many transactions or events which *may* have been involved in the creation of the intangible but with little scope for saying which specific events are associated with which specific item. For example, a brand will, in a general way, be the result of years of activity such as advertising, extra expenditure on raw materials to create a 'better than average' product, giving refunds to dissatisfied customers where there was no legal duty to do so, and so on. Each of these will have events or transactions associated with it but it will generally be impossible to link them directly to the future economic benefits embodied in the brand as it exists at any given moment. Thus the resolution of this issue turns on how the clause within the definition is interpreted.

We now turn to the treatment of intangibles under current GAAP. Until recently, GAAP contained relatively little on the subject but with the publication of FRS10 in 1997, systematic procedures are now documented. FRS10 was developed at a time when draft versions of the Statement of Principles were available and, in examining GAAP for intangibles, it is interesting to see how the accounting standard appears to have been influenced by the contents of the conceptual framework and to what extent GAAP can be regarded as approximating to the definition of assets in that framework. We will also be able to see how the application of the Statement of Principles is constrained by other influences such as company law.

FRS10 defines *intangible assets* as

non-financial fixed assets that do not have physical substance but are identifiable and are controlled by the entity through custody or legal rights.
(paragraph 2)

Strictly speaking, if we were following the Statement of Principles
rigidly, a term defined in this way should be called 'intangibles' or
'intangible items' rather than 'intangible *assets*' because it is possible that
things could satisfy this definition yet not satisfy the definition of, and
thus not be, assets.

Two terms used within the definition are themselves defined by
company law and are used here in the senses given by company law.
Fixed assets are assets that 'are intended for use on a continuing basis in
the company's activities' (CA, Section 262(1)). *Identifiable assets* are
defined as 'assets . . . which are capable of being disposed of . . . separately, without disposing of a business of the undertaking' (CA, Schedule
4A, paragraph 9(2)).[8] Defining intangible assets as fixed assets corresponds roughly to the notion that they generate benefits by their use in
the business rather than by being sold in the normal course of trade, and
excludes prepayments, which are current assets. The legal definition of
indentifiability is rather narrower than the notion we used earlier. It
might be possible to imagine, for example, a business revolving around a
single brand, where: (a) it was possible to identify the brand separately
as an intangible (using the ordinary sense of the word); (b) the brand did
satisfy the definition of an asset in the Statement of Principles; and (c)
the brand could not be sold separately from the business, especially if the
brand was based not only on advertising but also, for example, on
unique production facilities such as a source of mineral water. Under
these circumstances, the brand could satisfy the definition of an asset in
the Statement of Principles but would not satisfy the definition of an
intangible asset in FRS10 – and thus could not be a GAAP asset.

Clearly the use of the phrase 'controlled by the entity through custody
or legal rights' echoes wording in the Statement of Principles' definition.
However there are subtle differences between the two. In FRS10, control
is over the item rather than access to future economic benefits; thus it
would be possible to control a patent (which could thus satisfy the FRS10
definition of an intangible asset) when access to the future economic
benefits embodied in it were not controlled by the entity, perhaps
because the product was now banned on health grounds (so that it failed
the Statement of Principles' definition of an asset).

Again, the FRS10 definition allows for control *only* by custody or legal
rights whereas, under the approach of the Statement of Principles, these
are only examples of ways in which control could be exercised. However, the number of cases which fall between the two definitions is
probably very low.

The treatment of intangibles under FRS10 depends on whether they have been purchased or generated internally, that is, built up by the business itself. A brand, for example, can be developed internally by undertaking advertising, spending more on production to raise quality, promoting the brand via sponsorship, and so on. Alternatively rights to use the brand can be purchased from the previous owner.

FRS10 requires that intangibles purchased separately be capitalized and that those acquired as part of the purchase of a business be capitalized separately if they can be measured reliably, and capitalized as part of goodwill if not. An internally generated intangible may be capitalized (free choice) only if it has a readily ascertainable market value. The tests of reliable measurement and a readily ascertainable market value can be thought of as applying recognition criteria to the definition, and we will examine these in Chapter 7.

Overall, then, the approach of FRS10 can be thought of as an approximation to implementing the definition of assets in the Statement of Principles. The discrepancies between the two approaches are (GAAP is given first):

1   separate disposal versus separate identification, using identification in the ordinary sense of the word
2   control over the item versus control over access to future economic resources
3   control by custody or legal rights only versus custody or legal rights as examples of control over access to future economic benefits
4   free choice for internally generated intangibles subject to recognition criteria versus no free choice.

Operating costs of unused capacity on start-up

In some industries, it is necessary to create new capacity in fixed, relatively large, amounts and to meet most or all of the costs of running that capacity from the time at which it becomes operational, yet difficult or impossible to make full use of that capacity immediately. The classic example here is the hotel industry: it will take some time for a new hotel to build up custom to the point at which it is regularly fully booked, yet if it seeks to economize in the early days, for example by recruiting only a skeleton staff or failing to heat sections of the building, it is likely to discourage custom and, perhaps, never reach full capacity. Hence, it is accepted in these industries that new capacity will run at a loss for some period.

Until very recently, it was sometimes argued that GAAP permitted some part of the cost of unused capacity on start-up (*start-up costs*) to be capitalized. The cost of this unused capacity was generally identified in some way based on the loss incurred during the start-up period. The fundamental accounting concept of prudence, of course, limited the extent to which losses could be capitalized in this way (SSAP2 and CA).

FRS15, issued in 1999, deals with tangible fixed assets. It makes a distinction between:

(a) the commissioning period for plant, in which it is impossible for it to operate at normal levels because of, for example, the need to run in machinery, to test equipment and generally to ensure the proper functioning of the plant; and

(b) an initial operating period in which, although the plant is available for use and capable of running at normal levels, it is operated at below normal levels because demand has not yet built up. (paragraph 15)

Under FRS15, costs of the former but not the latter are to be included in the cost of the plant (paragraphs 14 and 16). Thus start-up costs of the sort outlined earlier cannot be capitalized. Does this treatment follow as a direct consequence of the definition of assets in the Statement of Principles?

The argument in favour of capitalizing start-up costs is based on the view that they are an inevitable cost of getting to a break-even level of operation, unavoidable just as the cost of building the hotel is unavoidable. They are thus part of the expenses that must be met from initial capital before a return is achieved and, because they are expected in advance, it would be misleading to report them as operating losses and imply that the new capacity was somehow under-performing.

But are start-up costs assets? Those who argue against capitalization stress that the losses do not in themselves give rise to future economic benefits: people stay in a hotel because it has a pleasant building and an attractive swimming pool but not because it has incurred previous trading losses. Hence start-up costs cannot satisfy the definition of assets and, because the system of definitions is comprehensive, cannot be included in the balance sheet and must be charged in the profit and loss account in the year in which they are incurred.

Arguments that this treatment is sound (and thus, by implication, that the definition of assets has assisted us to get to a sensible position on accounting for start-up costs) include: (a) we would not know when to stop capitalizing losses; (b) capitalization leads to a situation in which the worse the entity does in its initial trading, the better the balance sheet looks; (c) break-even may never be reached, leading to a position in which there are no revenues against which to charge the capitalized start-up costs and no way of securing the economic benefits which are supposed to be embodied in an asset (if the hotel makes losses permanently, the economic benefits embodied in the building can be secured by selling the building); (d) the entity can explain to users that the losses were expected and are normal in the industry concerned and leave it to them to decide how to treat the explanation (see Tweedie, 1996).

The argument that start-up costs are not, in themselves, assets under the definition in the Statement of Principles carries some considerable force. An alternative approach would be to argue that they were part of the initial or capital cost of the project of which they were part – say a hotel – and, in a cost-based measurement system like historical cost, could thus be capitalized as part of the cost of the project. This would have some force in terms of the economic substance of the business, though there remain all the problems of determining what constitutes the legitimate minimum cost of getting to the point at which the project is fully functioning (by contrast with costs of running the project inefficiently, which should, of course, be charged to the profit and loss account in the period). However, as long as elements of the balance sheet are established in terms of the *types* of items of property in which future economic benefits are embodied (land, buildings, plant, vehicles, stock, and so on), there is little scope for treating a project as an asset and thus no scope for including the initial costs of the project as the capitalized cost of an asset. Whether assets should be established in terms of projects is not a question that the definitions in the Statement of Principles help us solve. This question is related to the 'level of aggregation' problem discussed earlier.

Deferred operating expenditure

Some preparers argue that, subject to the concept of prudence, GAAP permits the capitalization of costs that would normally constitute operating expenditure when they are incurred in order to achieve future revenues, against which they can be matched. The arguments are similar to those set out in the previous section in relation to start-up costs.

Sometimes it is possible to view the expenditure as part of the cost of acquiring an item that does form the basis of an asset: for example the cost of programming staff time used to develop software internally can qualify under the definition of an asset. At the other extreme, some expenditure will be very unlikely to qualify under the definition. For example, an entity introducing new technology may have to make some staff redundant: while the cost of the redundancies is, for the entity, an inescapable cost of getting from the position it was previously in to one in which it can use the technology it is seeking to use, it is not an asset because the technology will not generate economic benefits as a result of the redundancies. This example illustrates how the Statement of Principles' definitions shift attention away from looking at the costs of doing things to asking whether what has resulted embodies future economic benefits.

Preliminary costs

Preliminary costs are the costs associated with setting up a new operating entity, for example a limited liability company. These costs include legal expenses, registration fees, costs of issuing capital, and so on. For an entity expecting to trade at a modest level for some period, preliminary expenses can represent a significant outgoing and historically it was customary to capitalize them, often referring to them as 'fictitious assets'. Current GAAP does not permit preliminary expenses to be carried on the balance sheet as an asset (CA, Schedule 4, paragraph 3(2)) and the Statement of Principles' definition of an asset helps to explain why: no future economic benefits will flow to the entity specifically as a result of the preliminary expenses it has incurred. Preliminary expenses can be thought of as a special case of start-up costs (see above) in which the project is the whole portfolio of activities to be undertaken by the entity.

Premium on redemption of debt

Suppose that a company issues £1 million of loan capital, repayable in 20 years' time, at a fixed rate of interest of 10% per year. The loan capital is traded on a stock exchange. Interest rates do not change for the first five years. Throughout that time the carrying amount of the loan capital will be £1 million and interest payments of £100,000 a year will be charged in the profit and loss account. At the end of the fifth year interest rates generally fall to 8% and as a result the market value of the loan capital rises – say to £1,250,000.[9] The company may choose to repurchase the loan capital in the market, cancel (redeem) it, and issue fresh loan capital. The new loan capital will bear interest at 8% and thus the profit and loss account from the sixth year onwards will include an interest charge of only £80,000, compared with £100,000 when the original loan was in place. There is a difference of £250,000 between the carrying amount of the redeemed debt (£1 million) and the cost of acquiring it. How should this premium be reflected in the financial statements?

Until 1993, GAAP permitted two alternative treatments. One treatment was to include the premium as an expense in the profit and loss account for the period in which the redemption took place. Under the alternative treatment, the premium was deferred and amortized over a number of future periods, that is, included in the profit and loss account in instalments over a number of periods. The argument for this treatment is that although the company paid a premium on redemption as a result of the change in interest rates, it is now enjoying the lower rate. If it issued loan capital with a life of 15 years to replace the original capital, it could charge the premium to the profit and loss account over the 15 years at £16,666 per year, thereby going some way to offset the decreased interest costs of £20,000 resulting from the lower rate applying to the new loan.

Under this alternative treatment the unamortized premium yet to be deducted from profit had to be carried forward on the balance sheet as a

GAAP asset. Does it qualify as an asset under the Statement of Principles? Although the company is now paying a lower interest rate than hitherto, it is not paying a lower rate than any other company that raised loan capital at the time that the refinancing was carried out and hence the premium does not yield future economic benefits and thus does not qualify as an asset. This position is reflected in current GAAP (FRS4, paragraph 32), which requires that the premium is charged as an expense in the year in which repurchase or settlement is made.

Executory contracts

A contract is, at the simplest, an agreement between two parties under which each performs actions in return for actions performed by the other. Classically, a purchase contract is an agreement by a supplier to provide goods or services in return for payment by the customer. Under certain circumstances, both parties to a contract may perform the actions involved in stages, as in a purchase contract under which the supplier supplies, and the customer pays for, goods in separate batches phased through time. An *executory contract* is one which is proportionally unperformed by the parties to the contract, that is 'both parties to the contract have still to perform to an equal degree the actions promised by and required of them under the contract' (SP, 4.36). In other words, either (a) neither party has performed any of the actions required under the contract (a wholly unperformed executory contract); or (b) both parties have performed some of the actions required and the actions performed are proportionate to each other, leaving unperformed actions also in equal degrees (a partially unperformed executory contract). A simple example of a partially unperformed executory contract would be one for the sale of two batches of supplies, where one batch had been supplied and paid for and the other had been neither supplied nor paid for.

The traditional position in financial reporting is that executory contracts are not recognized in financial statements. Thus, for example, if an entity places an order for raw materials, nothing will be entered in the primary financial records at the time of the order (though some memorandum record of the order should, of course, be kept). If, at the balance sheet date, the goods have been neither delivered nor paid for, nothing will appear in the balance sheet. Once the goods have been delivered they will appear in the balance sheet as stock and a corresponding creditor will appear under liabilities until the debt has been settled.

Two justifications for the traditional treatment of executory contracts are offered. The first is that, until one party or the other has performed its obligations under the contract, the other can usually cancel the contract without paying compensation. Thus, for example, the customer can cancel its purchase order for raw materials and escape any duty to pay for them. Equally, the supplier can say that it will not be able to fulfil the order, and it will not have to compensate the customer, merely having to go without the payment it would have received had it delivered the goods. Thus, goes the argument, an executory contract is subject to cancellation by either party without penalty and hence neither party can rely on its being performed. In the words of the Statement of Principles' definition of assets, and viewing the contract from the standpoint of the customer, access to the future economic benefits that might flow from the use of the raw materials to manufacture goods for subsequent sale are not under the entity's control and hence they do not qualify as an asset.

The second justification is that, under historical cost accounting, entering into the contract in itself has a zero cost. As long as it is possible to escape from the contract without compensation it is appropriate to continue not to recognize it, which may, indeed, be thought of as recognizing it at a carrying amount of nil. Should circumstances change so that it ceases to be possible to escape from the contract without loss, it may be necessary to recognize the amount of the loss as a provision (the contract would become an *onerous contract* under FRS12, paragraphs 71–4).

The definition in the Statement of Principles invites us to look again at the nature and treatment of executory contracts. Many such contracts will indeed be unenforceable routine purchase arrangements, in that both parties will be able to escape their obligations without penalty, either because the terms of the contract permit this or because, even though the contract gives rise to obligations in law, in practice each party would find it more costly to enforce these than to abandon its rights. Under these circumstances, it may well be that an entity placing an order does not control access to the economic benefits that would flow from delivery of the order, and thus does not have an asset.

However, many executory contracts will not necessarily fall into this category. We can look at three examples. So-called 'take-or-pay contracts' are agreements under which an entity commits itself to purchasing at least a minimum quantity of goods or services, usually over a stated period and usually for a price specified in the agreement. The customer agrees to pay for the minimum quantity, whether or not it takes delivery of that quantity.[10] The incentive to do so is that it obtains a guaranteed line of supply and a lower price than if it places its orders in batches. The supplier is, of course, entitled in law to enforce the contract and is often likely to do so, partly because it may have turned away other orders or incurred expenditure in expanding capacity, and partly because it has a powerful incentive to do so. The customer is also entitled to enforce the contract and thus obtain the economic benefits that will flow from using the supplies.

The second example is a 'throughput contract'. This is an arrangement under which one party agrees to pay a fixed amount to another in return for using a facility for up to a stated level of service (for example for using an oil pipeline to transport up to a stated quantity of oil or for a stated period). The amount will be paid regardless of the actual usage made of the facility (within any agreed maximum). Again both parties have legal powers to enforce the contract and considerable incentives to do so.

The third example is the case where, under a routine purchase arrangement, the circumstances are such as to give at least one party, say the purchaser, control over access to the future economic benefits. This might come about under a contract for the supply of a single batch of material where either (a) the terms of the contract state that the purchaser can effectively enforce delivery and the use it will make of the material is so profitable that it will have a powerful incentive to do so; or (b) the purchaser is a large and regular customer of the supplier so that the supplier has a substantial commercial incentive not to break the contract.

In all three cases, the entity purchasing the goods or services may have effective control over access to the economic benefits expected to flow from the contract, either in the form of acquiring and using those goods or services or by obtaining compensation. There is a past event, namely the signing of the contract. Hence it would appear that the contract could give rise to an asset under the Statement of Principles' definition. It would also, of course, give rise to an associated liability, namely the obligation to pay for the goods or services when delivered, so the net impact on the balance sheet total from incorporating the contract in the balance sheet would be nil.

As explained above, at the moment GAAP does not record executory contracts in the financial statements unless the obligation comes to exceed the benefits, for example because the prices of the entity's finished goods fall to the point at which it will not be able to use the goods or services it is contracted to purchase profitably. If that occurs, what will be recognized is the *net* amount of the loss to be incurred rather than amounts for the asset and liability separately.[11] The US conceptual framework invites us to look closely at what is happening here (SFAC6, paragraphs 251–3). Take, for example, the case where a company orders goods for resale and the price in the retail market falls after an irrevocable order has been placed but not yet delivered. The amount of the obligation (to pay the contract price to the supplier) does not *increase*; rather the loss currently recognized under US and UK GAAP is conceptually a valuation account adjusting the amount of the *asset*. However, because, unlike most other valuation accounts (for example depreciation and the provision for bad debts), the corresponding asset is not shown on the balance sheet, it has to be included as an increase in liabilities. It is shown in this way even though liabilities have not in fact increased.

One of the difficulties that results from the Statement's use of a set of definitions which presumes that the underlying items to be tested have been identified, without explaining how this is to be done, is that when we encounter a 'mixed bundle' of benefits and obligations (disbenefits), it is not clear when we should look at the bundle overall, identifying a potential asset or liability from the net position, and when we should unbundle the streams to look for individual assets and liabilities. There is nothing in the system of definitions as such that points unambiguously to netting off executory contracts, although the Statement does argue that this will be appropriate under its approach (SP, 4.35–6). This does not accord with the treatment of finance leases or the comments of the US conceptual framework quoted above.

It is instructive to ask why it should matter whether assets and liabilities under an executory contract should be shown separately or netted off. One answer would be that if we have a system of definitions we should follow them consistently and two items that possess the same characteristics in relation to those definitions should be treated in the same way. If this does not happen, users of the information may be confused and there is also something wrong with the system of definitions because they are not, in fact, proving definitive: something else is influencing whether items are being treated as assets or not. At a minimum, we need an unambiguous, conceptually derived, model of netting.

Another answer would look to the usefulness of the financial statements in the light of the objective of those statements adopted by the Statement of Principles. Recognition of executory contracts in gross terms and recognition in net terms both have the same impact on ownership interest (because of the way it is defined) and both will indicate the current amount of any loss under the contract. However, the net presentation will not give users information about the economic benefits, access to which the entity controls as a result of entering into the contract, and in this way the presentation is less informative than that in the case where the entity has taken delivery of stock but has yet to pay for it. Equally, the net presentation will not give users information about the entity's exposure to possible losses if the economic benefits are not in fact obtained but payment must nonetheless be made: again, in this way the presentation is less informative than the case where the entity has taken delivery of stock but has yet to pay for it.[12]

Appealing to the usefulness of information is not the final arbiter of accounting policy decisions under the approach of the Statement of Principles: accounting policy choices should be made on the basis of the principles set out in the Statement,[13] which themselves are derived from a consideration of the usefulness of alternative ways of doing things. Nonetheless, where there are ambiguities in those principles, going back to the objective of financial statements may help to clarify their application.

Goodwill

As we have already seen, the Statement of Principles approaches the determination of what satisfies the definition of an asset by starting with the 'items' embodying future economic benefits. Thus the test of control is applied to individual items: can the entity ensure that it obtains the future economic benefits embodied in a debtor, or a piece of stock or machinery? It may be that some future economic benefits attach to the entity itself, rather than to items that can be identified separately from it. We have seen that the Statement of Principles gives as examples here, market share, superior management and good labour relations. The entity cannot choose when to obtain those benefits within the business and cannot realize them by sale because they cannot be separated from the business. Hence the benefits can be obtained only by selling the entity as a whole and thus the entity itself does not control them. The factors discussed here, and others like them, are generally taken to underlie what accountants refer to as goodwill, that is the excess of the value of a business over the value of its individual assets less liabilities. To be slightly more precise, we can define goodwill as the excess of the value of a business over the value of its individual assets less liabilities after correcting for: (a) items that do qualify as assets but which have been omitted from the balance sheet; (b) failure to reflect assets at fair value; and (c) errors in the valuation of the business as a whole, for example if an excessively high price has been paid for it during the course of a contested takeover. This, more precise, notion can be referred to as core goodwill (Johnson and Petrone, 1998). According to the Statement of Principles (SP, 4.21), core goodwill fails the 'control' test, and thus is not an asset of the entity.

Current GAAP (FRS10) distinguishes between internally generated goodwill (where the value of a business has come to exceed that of its individual assets) and purchased goodwill (where this gap is explicit because a business has been acquired by another so that its assets now appear on the acquirer group's balance sheet, and the difference between the cost of the acquisition and the carrying amounts of the individual assets less liabilities must be dealt with in some way on the consolidation). There is no difference in principle between the two types of goodwill. Current GAAP requires that internally generated goodwill should not be capitalized but that purchased goodwill should be capitalized, that is, treated as an asset. This latter treatment was adopted by the ASB as recently as 1997 (that is, after the Statement of Principles had been issued as a draft by the ASB). It was adopted despite the ASB's apparent view that purchased goodwill does not qualify as an asset and this point is made explicitly in FRS10:

> goodwill arising on an acquisition is neither an asset like other assets nor an immediate loss in value . . . Although purchased goodwill is not in itself an asset, its inclusion among the assets of the reporting entity, rather than as a deduction from shareholders' equity, recognises that goodwill is part of a larger asset, the investment, for which management remains accountable. (paragraph b)

The same point is made – in more or less the same terms – in the Statement of Principles (SP, 8.13).

FASB have examined the question of whether core goodwill is an asset according to their definition (Johnson and Petrone, 1998). They reached the conclusion that it *does* satisfy their definition. Their definition is as follows:

> Assets are probable future economic benefits obtained or controlled by a particular entity as a result of past transactions or events. (SFAC6, paragraph 25)

The principal differences between the two definitions concern whether uncertainty is dealt with explicitly in the definition and whether the need for access to the benefits is explicitly referred to. Neither of these two differences appears immediately to explain why the two standard-setters have reached opposite conclusions on this fundamental issue.

The FASB's reasoning is set out in Johnson and Petrone (1988). For the FASB core goodwill, though it cannot be sold by the entity or used to settle liabilities, does yield future economic benefits because, in combination with other assets, it contributes indirectly to the generation of cash flows which will be higher than they would be if the goodwill did not exist. Purchased core goodwill is, for the FASB, controlled as a result of the acquirer's controlling interest in the acquiree and there is a past transaction, namely the acquisition itself.

The ASB appears to accept that there are future economic benefits associated with core goodwill but argues that the entity does not control access to them, independently of the business as a whole, because 'it is generally not possible for an entity to choose if and when to realise the economic benefits derivable from factors such as its market share, superior management or good labour relations' (SP, 4.21). Two objections may be raised to this line of reasoning. First, the definition does not require that access to future economic benefits be controlled independently for each asset or independently of control over the business, but only that it be controlled. Secondly, businesses clearly have some measure of control over access to the benefits of, say, market share in that they can stop spending the additional resources that have secured this position, exploit the position by maximizing short-term prices, and thereby increase short-term profit while running the risk of losing market share. In this way they can 'realize' the benefit by disposing of it for higher profits. The degree of control involved here is arguably as great as that over the economic benefits associated with a newly invented drug.

We need not attempt to resolve this dispute between the UK and the USA about how to interpret conceptual frameworks that do not, themselves, appear to be significantly different. The lesson for us is that interpretation is itself a complicated business and by no means easy. Critics would say that this incident shows that conceptual frameworks do not actually help with standard-setting because the difficult problems simply throw up a range of interpretations to support the various positions participants in the process wish to take. However, the framework does serve, even in this case, to sharpen the focus on what issues need to be addressed.

Notes

1 Satisfying the definition of one of the elements is a necessary but not a sufficient condition for inclusion in the financial statements: an item must also meet other tests, as described in Chapter 7.

2 The fourth edition of Parker, published in 1994, gave a definition much closer to that of the Statement of Principles.

3 Because of the potential existence of assets such as those described in this and the preceding paragraph, the Statement of Principles is, strictly speaking, oversimplifying when it says that 'future economic benefits eventually result in net cash inflows to the entity' (SP, 4.15).

4 And assuming that the benefits associated with the warehouse exceed its cost so that no impairment provision is necessary under the aggregate approach.

5 Whether they are correctly classified under current GAAP is another, though less significant, matter. See Chapter 9.

6 The new approach to accounting for leases is the subject of an ASB Discussion Paper, *Leases: Implementation of a New Approach*, issued in December 1999.

7 The tests also address recognition criteria: see Chapter 7.

8 The CA definition actually covers identifiable assets and liabilities and thus some words are redundant when looking only at assets.

9 Lenders now have to invest £1,250,000 to receive annual interest payments of £100,000 (£1,250,000 at 8%) and thus will be prepared to pay this amount for the company's loan capital since it will generate the equivalent in interest. The difference in value of the return of principal in 15 years' time is ignored.

10 The term 'take-or-pay' is thus highly misleading: the choice in fact is not 'take *or* pay' but rather 'take or don't take as you prefer but pay anyway'.

11 Under certain circumstances a throughput contract can constitute a finance lease and be required to be brought onto the balance sheet under SSAP21.

12 The literature of accounting theory has included calls for the economic benefits under executory contracts to be eligible for consideration as assets for over half a century: see, for example, Canning (1929).

13 Strictly speaking, in accordance with accounting standards derived from the principles set out in the Statement.

References

Bromwich, M. (1989) 'A decision required on decision-oriented accounting', in G. Macdonald and B.A. Rutherford (eds), *Accounts, Accounting and Accountability*. London: Van Nostrand Reinhold and Institute of Chartered Accountants in England and Wales. pp. 47–60.

Canning, J.B. (1929) *The Economics of Accounting*. New York: Ronald.

Carsberg, B., Arnold, J. and Hope, A. (1977) 'Predictive value: a criterion of choice of accounting method', in W.T. Baxter and S. Davidson (eds), *Studies in*

Accounting. London: Institute of Chartered Accountants in England and Wales. pp. 403–23.

Davies, M., Paterson, R. and Wilson, A. (1999) *UK GAAP*, 6th edn. London: Macmillan.

Johnson, L.T. and Petrone, K.R. (1998) 'Is goodwill an asset?', *Accounting Horizons*, September: 293–303.

McGregor, W. (1996) *Accounting for Leases: a New Approach.* Norwalk, CT: Financial Accounting Standards Board.

Parker, R.H. (1988) *Understanding Company Financial Statements*, 3rd edn. London: Penguin.

Sterling, R.R. (1970) 'On theory construction and verification', *Accounting Review*, July: 444–57.

Tweedie, D. (1996) 'Regulating change: the role of the conceptual statement in standard setting', in I. Lapsley and F. Mitchell (eds), *Accounting and Performance Measurement.* London: Paul Chapman. pp. 18–34.

Weetman, P. (1999) *Financial Accounting: an Introduction*, 2nd edn. London: Financial Times and Prentice-Hall.

Further reading

For a discussion of the FASB's view of goodwill, see L.T. Johnson and K.R. Petrone, 'Is goodwill an asset?', *Accounting Horizons*, September 1998, pp. 293–303.

For an analysis of the nature of operating leases, see W. McGregor, *Accounting for Leases: a New Approach*, Norwalk, CT: Financial Accounting Standards Board, 1996.

See also the further reading for Chapter 6.

5

Elements of Financial
Statements II: Liabilities

As we saw in Chapter 4, the Statement of Principles' system of element definitions is tightly integrated and places assets at the heart of the system. Liabilities are the mirror image of assets.

The nature of liabilities

The Statement of Principles defines liabilities in the following terms:

> Liabilities are obligations of an entity to transfer economic benefits as a result of past transactions or events. (SP, 4.23)

As with assets, this definition is expressed in economic terms. Liabilities involve the transfer of economic benefits and arise when an entity will have to make such a transfer, regardless of whether it has a strict legal duty to do so. The concept of a liability adopted by the Statement of Principles follows from the Statement's approach to users and their information needs. As we have seen, users need to evaluate an entity's ability to generate surpluses and associated net cash inflows (including the timing and risk involved). Liabilities affect the entity's ability to generate cash because they represent claims on the entity's resources: resources used to meet liabilities will, as a result, not be available thereafter to generate cash for the entity or be distributed to its owners. Hence, in evaluating an entity's ability to generate cash from its resource base, users will need to take into account, and thus be given information about, the liabilities that will have to be met from that base.

Attributes of liabilities

Obligations

An essential attribute of a liability is an *obligation* to transfer economic benefits. It is not essential that the transfer is certain but it is essential that there is an obligation and that it might result in the transfer of benefits. Thus a legal duty to make a payment to a creditor is a liability even if there is some doubt about whether the creditor will press the claim.

An obligation to make a transfer arises when the entity is not free to avoid making the transfer. In certain circumstances, the entity may believe that it has good grounds for persuading the party to which it is obligated to forgo settlement, but unless it is in a position to insist on this, it remains under an obligation. Equally, as explained in the previous paragraph, doubt about whether the other party will enforce its rights does not alter the position that there is an obligation.

The most common source of an obligation will be legal rights of a third party to insist on a transfer of economic resources, for example as payment for goods or services supplied to the entity under a contract. However, obligations can arise from other sources to create *constructive* obligations. For example, in a particular situation, an entity may have the legal right to decline to make a transfer but consider that to do so would have consequences which would be commercially more damaging than the cost of the transfer. This might be the case where a retailer adopts a policy of providing refunds for returned goods even where there is no legal duty to do so, in order to enhance its reputation and build customer loyalty: the damage to its reputation from refusing refunds might substantially exceed the cost of granting them. Thus, at any particular point in time, it has a constructive obligation to provide refunds for goods returned from past sales, as and when they are claimed. Another example would be employee benefits routinely paid without any legal duty to do so under a contract of employment, such as an annual bonus. Past practice creates an expectation that such payments will be made and failure to do so without due warning may lower morale and create industrial relations problems that would cost the company more than the amount of the bonus: hence once the event that normally triggers a bonus has occurred there may be a constructive obligation to pay it.

However, it is important to appreciate that an entity does not *come under an obligation* merely by deciding that it would be a good idea, or even in its interests, to transfer economic benefits, or even by actually deciding that it will transfer benefits. Thus, for example, when an entity decides to build a new factory it will not usually, as a result of that decision itself, come under an obligation. This will be true even if there is a formal decision of the board of directors. This is because the entity could reverse its decision to build the factory and thereby avoid any transfer of economic benefits: it will neither have to make the transfers that would follow from the building of the factory (paying the construction company, and so on) nor have to compensate anyone for changing its decision.

Obligations arise, then, not as a result of the decision but as the decision is implemented and the entity purchases land, enters into contracts for the construction of buildings and so on. The entity may create constructive obligations prior to taking on strict legal duties, for example by making public announcements about its intentions, perhaps causing other parties to vary their behaviour, so that it would find it commercially damaging to reverse its decision. The point at which a decision, which does not itself create legal obligations, comes to represent a constructive obligation, for example by creating general expectations that it will be implemented, will often be difficult to identify in practice.

Transfer of economic benefits

The transfer of economic benefits that is involved in settling liabilities may come about in a variety of ways. The most common is, of course, payment in cash. Other ways in which liabilities are settled include: (a) the transfer of resources other than cash; (b) delivery of services (as where they have been prepaid); (c) incurring another liability (for example taking out a fresh loan from the same bank to refinance an existing loan); (d) offset against assets held by the entity in the form of debts due from the party to which the liability is owed; and (e) cancellation by the party to which the obligation is owed (for example where government waives a charge as a matter of public policy).

Entities commonly engage in transactions which give rise to both an asset and a liability, as when goods are received on credit. This does not mean that the acquisition of an asset automatically implies that a liability has been incurred. For example receipt of cash may be associated with: (a) payment of a debt owed to the entity (reduction in another asset); (b) a cash sale (reduction of another asset); or (c) a contribution from the owner (increase in ownership interest).

Past transactions or events

The obligation to transfer economic benefits must result from past transactions or other events. For example, in the straightforward case of an amount owed to a supplier, the obligation results from goods or services having been delivered. If a series of transactions or events must take place before an obligation is incurred, whether or not an obligation exists at any particular point in time will require examination of whether any of the relevant transactions or events are still under the entity's control. For example, if the entity's contract with its supplier allows orders to be cancelled without penalty prior to delivery, and given that entities do not normally have an obligation to pay for goods delivered to them which they have not ordered, an obligation to pay for a particular batch of goods will arise only after the entity has *both* ordered the goods and received them. Placing an order does not result in an obligation because the entity can subsequently cancel the order; equally delivery does not result in an obligation (or an asset) unless an order has already been placed or the entity agrees to keep the goods nonetheless.

The requirement for there to be 'past transactions or events' to justify the treatment of an item as a liability parallels that relating to assets. As with assets, this clause is best seen as underlining the requirement that an obligation must actually exist rather than being a separate requirement in its own right.

Other aspects of the definition

Uncertainty

The amount of the transfer of economic benefits, and, indeed, whether it will take place at all, may be uncertain. One entity may guarantee the debts of another – usually an associated business – and, at any given date, the probability of the second entity failing, so that the guarantee is taken up, may be very small. This is an example of a liability which is unlikely to have to be settled at all. Nonetheless, the guarantee gives rise to a liability for the guarantor because, if circumstances mean that a claim is made, the guarantor cannot escape the obligation to transfer economic resources to the entity holding the guarantee.[1] Many obligations, especially constructive obligations, are of uncertain amount. Examples include those expressed in terms of services to be provided, such as warranties to repair goods, those resulting from legal cases for damages, and those expressed in foreign currencies. In some cases the potential recipient of the amount may also be uncertain or unknown, as in the case of refunds under warranties. Uncertainty does not affect whether an obligation (and thus a liability) exists but it will influence the recognition and measurement of the liability (see Chapters 7 and 8).

Offsetting

An entity will usually engage in a large number of transactions and events, each of which may have given rise to a number of rights and obligations. The question arises as to how the individual rights and obligations springing from the totality of these transactions and events should be combined, if at all, before determining whether an item satisfies the definition of an asset or a liability. For example, suppose an entity supplies goods to another party to the value of £100,000, while at the same time borrowing £60,000 from that other party, which might, perhaps, be a bank. Does the entity have (a) an asset of £100,000 (the amount due to it as a result of the supply of goods) and an obligation of £60,000 (the duty to repay the loan); or (b) an asset of £40,000 (the net amount receivable from the other party)? The act of netting off the two amounts is referred to in the Statement of Principles as *offsetting*.

The approach taken in the Statement of Principles is that if receivables and payables exist and the reporting entity has an assured ability to insist on the net settlement of the balances, then the balances constitute a single asset or liability of the net amount and this is so whether or not the entity intends to settle the amounts in this way. Thus if the entity is in a position to require net settlement, and this does not depend on any party or event outside the entity's control, there is a single asset or liability. The way in which the amount will actually be settled does not affect the position. This approach follows because, where the reporting entity can insist on net settlement, there is no obligation beyond the amount of any net liability: if the net balance is an asset, there is no obligation on the reporting entity at all.

However, any other position, such as a general understanding between two parties that mutual debts will be settled by set-off but without an enforceable arrangement, does not give rise to offsetting of the assets and liabilities involved. The implication of the approach is that non-monetary assets cannot be involved in offsetting.

Because offsetting of separate assets and liabilities is not permitted, they must be shown separately and not combined. This is logically necessary because they each satisfy the definition of an element and must be treated as such: the underlying rationale follows from the needs of users to be given information about the entity's resource base and claims upon that base, rather than merely its net financial position.

Interest

The normal basis on which commercial enterprises undertake business with each other in a developed economy means that many liabilities, especially those not due for settlement in the short term, will carry a duty to pay interest as recompense for the time value of money. However, the absence of a duty to pay interest does not, in itself, mean that an arrangement is not a liability, even where settlement is not due for a considerable period after the originating transaction.

Valuation accounts

As with assets, the amount of a liability may need to be adjusted after its initial incorporation in the balance sheet. For example a loan repayable at a premium, presumably because the associated rate of interest is lower than the market rate, will need to be increased to the amount repayable. The adjustment is not, in itself, a liability but rather a valuation account adjusting the carrying amount of the initial liability. In the same way, if the loan was repayable at a discount, the adjustment would not be an asset but a valuation account. Although they are less common than the equivalent valuation accounts for assets (depreciation, provisions for bad debts, and so on), the principle is the same.

Credit entries in the balance sheet

The comprehensive nature of the Statement of Principles' system of definitions of financial statement elements means that all credit entries in the balance sheet must take one of two forms: (a) liabilities; or (b) ownership interest. Since ownership interest is defined in terms of assets less liabilities (see Chapter 6), it follows that the definition of liabilities is crucial in determining not only what is classified as liabilities but also what is classified as ownership interest: all credit entries to be carried forward via the balance sheet that do not satisfy the definition of liabilities must be classified as ownership interest.

Criticisms of the definition

Some commentators criticize the definition of liabilities as part of an attack on the whole structure of the element definitions and we will examine these criticisms in Chapter 6. Those who accept the broad approach of the Statement of Principles point to two principal problem areas.

The first is the need, under the definition, for there to be at least a constructive obligation to transfer future economic benefits. This clause prohibits entities from 'earmarking' amounts to cover such future outflows as (a) expenditure on restructuring business units, even where these are currently failing; (b) upgrading capacity to remain competitive; (c) long-term maintenance; or (d) future losses to be incurred by 'start-up' businesses, even where such losses are an inevitable consequence of moving into a business area where it is impossible realistically to trade profitability from the first day, so that some period of build-up is necessary. In each case, a company (specifically, its directors) may feel that it has a powerful commitment to go through with the proposed course of action, either to survive or to earn future profits from a new area.

However, under the Statement of Principles, until actual obligations arise there are no liabilities. In the first three cases, the company could change its decision – and suffer the consequences. Equally, although the future trading losses in the start-up situation may be inevitable, they will result from future trading transactions not a past obligation.

Some commentators feel that the fundamental accounting concept of prudence should come into play here. A company intending to restructure, upgrade or maintain its infrastructure should at least be permitted, as a matter of prudence, to provide in advance for these actions. Equally, a company consciously deciding to pursue a course of action that will yield short-term losses under contemporary accounting practice should at least be permitted to provide for them. We have already examined the arguments against permitting prudence to introduce bias into the financial statements (see Chapter 3). We will examine some specific cases of this argument at greater length later in this chapter.

The second principal problem is the difficulty of drawing the line between liabilities and ownership interest, which, as explained earlier, turns exclusively on the definition of liabilities. Examples of this problem are discussed in Chapter 5.

Although there are, in principle, difficulties in identifying an individual liability, paralleling those arising in the case of individual assets, they are less apparent in practice. This is because liabilities are essentially non-physical.

One practical problem with the definition is the difficulty of identifying when a constructive obligation comes into existence: we will examine this point in relation to restructuring later in this chapter but it arises also in connection with other liabilities, for example for product warranties.

Applications of the definition

We will now examine how the Statement of Principles' definition of liabilities can be applied to a variety of items which might potentially be included as credit entries in an entity's balance sheet. As in our consideration of applications of the definition of assets, in straightforward cases our discussion illustrates the meaning of the definition while in more difficult cases the process of applying the definition can help in deciding what the appropriate accounting treatment of an item might be. Again, as in our consideration of assets, we are mildly handicapped by the shortage of terms to distinguish between: (a) the 'things' we actually encounter in business life (for example, loans); (b) the obligations that arise from those 'things'; (c) such of those obligations as satisfy the definition of liabilities in the Statement of Principles; (d) those items that qualify to be treated as liabilities under GAAP; and (e) classes or groups of 'things', obligations and liabilities. All these are commonly called liabilities. For the purposes of this discussion we will generally use *liability* for obligations satisfying the Statement of Principles' definition of that term, and *GAAP liability* for items that are permitted to be included in the balance sheet as liabilities under GAAP.

Borrowing

Loans, whether from banks or other parties, are arrangements under which the lender transfers cash or credit (that is, the means to make cash payments to third parties) to the entity. In the commercial world the arrangement usually involves a condition that interest is paid on outstanding amounts and that the principal is repaid. The repayment of principal may be at a fixed date, or over a fixed period, or become due when specified events occur, or may be at the discretion of the lender or borrower. In the case of perpetual bonds, the entity does not have an obligation to repay the principal (investors can liquidate their investment by selling their holding on to a third party) but it will generally have an obligation to pay interest.

The borrower will generally have an obligation to pay interest – and possibly to repay the principal – by transferring cash, or some cash equivalent such as commodities with a readily measurable market value, to the lender. This obligation arises as a result of a past transaction, namely the original loan. Hence loans will satisfy the definition of a liability. The obligation and the past transaction will be evidenced by the loan agreement.

The obligation to pay interest comes about with the passage of time rather than on the initial act of raising the loan. The 'past transactions or events' clause can be regarded as being triggered by the event of time passing, although, of course, both the initial receipt of the loan and the passage of time are necessary to make the interest itself an obligation.[2]

An entity opening a bank account will normally pay money into the account and will thereafter be permitted by the bank to issue cheques up to the amount of the balance paid in. While there is a credit balance in the account the entity has access to cash or the ability to pass that cash on to a third party and this will normally qualify as an asset. An overdraft facility is an arrangement whereby the bank agrees that the entity may issue cheques to a greater value than its credit balance, thereby taking the account into debit, on condition that the excess is restored by further credits in due course.

Once the entity begins to use this facility it acquires an obligation to repay the bank under the terms of its overdraft. This repayment will normally be achieved by paying into the account credits (such as cheques from customers) which it could otherwise use to obtain cash but which, because they have been paid into an account in overdraft, will not be available in this way. This amounts to transferring economic benefits to the bank. The obligation to make this transfer arises from the past transactions of issuing the cheques which resulted in the overdraft and thereby borrowing from the bank. Hence an overdraft will generally satisfy the definition of a liability.

It is possible in principle to imagine cases in which a loan or overdraft might not satisfy the definition of a liability, for example: (a) the 'lender' might give a watertight agreement, without recompense or compensation, to waive its right to repayment and interest; (b) the 'lender' might be punished for some misdemeanour by being banned from recovering the loan; or (c) it might no longer be possible to trace the 'lender' (say, if it was located in a foreign country) in circumstances in which it is possible to be confident that contact will not be re-established. The conditions in (a) occasionally arise and mean that the loan has effectively become a gift; the other circumstances described are extremely rare and practical examples of apparent loans which do not satisfy the definition of a liability must be virtually non-existent.

Trade creditors

Trade creditors represent an obligation to pay for goods and services received. They are usually settled by transfer of cash to the creditor but may occasionally be settled by other means such as offsetting against an amount due, replacement by another financing arrangement with the same entity, or the transfer of goods to the creditor. The past transaction or other event will usually be the receipt of the goods or services: strictly this may give rise only to a constructive obligation, with the legal obligation to settle the debt arising only after receipt of the invoice and, possible, the elapse of any period of credit granted by the supplier. Nonetheless, the constructive obligation is sufficient to meet the definition of a liability.

Prepayments

Businesses may require customers to pay for goods or services in advance or place a deposit to confirm their commitment to receiving and paying for the goods or services ordered. Under these circumstances an asset (usually cash) is received and GAAP treats this as matched by a liability to the customer. The supplier will indeed have an obligation, usually either to supply the goods or services or refund the deposit or prepayment, and both these actions involve the transfer of economic benefits to the customer: hence the amount satisfies the definition of a liability.[3]

Proposed dividends

Large quoted companies almost invariably include in their annual financial statements an amount to cover proposed dividends to the company's shareholders. Under current GAAP these are shown as GAAP liabilities.

The dividends will be the subject of a proposal from the directors to the shareholders and will be formally voted on at the company's annual general meeting. Until that vote is passed the company has no legal obligation to pay the dividend. The fact that the shareholders themselves have the opportunity to decide whether or not the dividend should proceed, and can refuse to authorize the dividend without penalty to the company (indeed, without penalty to themselves in that, as we have seen already, the larger retained profits will simply leave the share price higher), suggests that there is no constructive obligation.

As a consequence, it is normally considered that proposed dividends do not satisfy the definition of liabilities in the Statement of Principles and the Statement itself acknowledges that is an area in which current GAAP (and company law) is at odds with the conceptual framework (SP, Appendix I, paragraph 6).

Long-term infrastructural maintenance

Some businesses have large infrastructural assets which require occasional but very expensive programmes of maintenance. Examples here include blast furnace relining and the dry-docking of ships. Similar considerations arise where a large number of assets require occasional major overhauls, the total cost of which is substantial, as in the case of aircraft engines.

Until recently, GAAP permitted entities to build up amounts for the necessary maintenance by debiting the profit and loss account and crediting a provision in the balance sheet and this was, indeed, common practice. Under the Statement of Principles, the balance sheet can contain as credits only liabilities and ownership interest, and if the provision is to be a liability there must be an obligation to transfer economic benefits to another entity. This will generally not apply under the circumstances described here. The business may intend to carry through the maintenance but it is not under an obligation, even a constructive obligation, to do so. It can be argued that this will be the case even where there is a legal requirement, or one imposed by industry regulators, to carry out the maintenance if the business wishes to continue to use the assets – as is the case with aircraft engines. This is because the entity could choose to dispose of the assets, in their existing condition, and thereby avoid the cost of the overhaul, albeit by settling for a lower consideration. It could then continue in business by replacing the asset with one that had been maintained and it would be under no obligation to pay the higher amount for a maintained asset until it entered into a contract.

In general, it will be the case that the asset shows some level of progressive deterioration or other reduction in future economic benefits during the periods between the maintenance programmes. For example the blast furnace lining will deteriorate; and in the case of aircraft engines, where the requirement for an overhaul is generally based on the number of flying hours which have elapsed since the last overhaul, as flying hours increase the future economic benefits which can be obtained by using the engine to earn fare revenue without further overhaul will diminish. This deterioration, or the sacrifice of future economic benefits, is a cost of using the asset in the period in which it occurs and should thus be charged to the profit and loss account in that period. Yet the Statement of Principles will not allow us to record a liability: how is this circle to be squared?

The answer is very straightforward. The reduction in future economic benefits is a diminution in an asset, namely the blast furnace, aircraft engine or whatever, and not a liability, and it should be recognized by charging depreciation and thus showing it in the balance sheet as a valuation account (accumulated depreciation) under assets. When the maintenance is carried out it will restore the benefits embodied in the item and the expenditure can thus be capitalized as an adjustment to the carrying amount of the asset, as would occur if expenditure was incurred on enhancing the service potential of an asset in the normal way. This is now the treatment required by GAAP, as a result of the introduction of FRS12, which was clearly heavily influenced by the Statement of Principles, then in draft form.

The new treatment required by FRS12 will not affect the profit and loss account, except in cases where, under the old treatment, a provision was built up for some future maintenance but there was no current deterioration. This might be held to apply, for example, in cases where an entity leases a building under a lease which contains a requirement to refurbish the property every few years but, at any rate in the early years after one refurbishment, no real dilapidation has yet to manifest itself. Other than in those cases, the overall impact on the profit and loss account of the old and new treatments will be the same: an amount will be charged which previously would have been classified as a general expense and now will be shown in depreciation. Whereas before the carrying amount of the asset would decline over time in accordance with the chosen depreciation policy, now there will be two patterns: (a) a cyclical fall and rise reflecting the extent to which the need for maintenance erodes the asset and this erosion is then restored by maintenance; and (b) a steady decline in the carrying amount of the remainder of the asset which is not subject to the need for periodic maintenance, reflecting, as before, the application of the chosen depreciation policy. Critics of the ASB's conceptual framework regard this as undesirable: 'it may give rise to some very odd depreciation policies, with different parts of assets which are not separately distinguishable being depreciated over different lives' (Davies et al., 1999: 1693). The alternative view is that the changes in the carrying amount of the asset now better reflect the pattern in which the future economic benefits embodied in it are consumed by the entity.

Business restructuring

In today's dynamic business environment, companies frequently need to carry through substantial programmes of restructuring to change the focus of a major part of the company or the manner in which its activities are conducted. This restructuring may include the sale or termination of a line of business; the closure or relocation of business activities; and changes in management structure. A restructuring on this scale has a substantial impact on the financial statements. It is possible to include the effect of a restructuring, ahead of the outlays involved, by charging the cost in the profit and loss account and setting up a provision in the balance sheet. Given the impact on the financial statements, a critical issue here is the timing of the recognition of the provision.

Until recently, GAAP permitted a provision to be recognized once a clear decision had been taken to carry the restructuring out, for example in the form of a board decision, formally minuted. This was changed in 1998 by FRS12. The standard was heavily influenced by the Statement of Principles, then in draft form, as can be seen from the wording described here.

It contains a requirement that a provision be included in the balance sheet only when, among other things, 'an entity has a present obligation (legal or constructive) as a result of a past event' (paragraph 14). In the case of restructuring, the standard further provides that:

a constructive obligation to restructuring arises only when an entity:

(a)   has a detailed formal plan . . . and
(b)   has raised a valid expectation in those affected that it will carry out the restructuring by starting to implement that plan or announcing its main features to those affected by it. (paragraph 77)

The paragraph also lists a variety of matters which the formal plan must specify. The standard states quite specifically that a board decision does not, by itself, give rise to a constructive obligation. Put simply, board decisions can be reversed without penalty. There remains, however, a good deal of difficulty in determining exactly when a decision has given rise to a constructive obligation.

The new approach prevents companies that have decided to restructure (and have no desire to change the decision) from recognizing that decision immediately and could be argued to run against the principle of prudence. However, companies can, and do, change their minds about the scale and timing of restructurings, and occasionally about whether they are necessary at all, and the consequent release of unused provisions back to the profit and loss account can represent a significant form of managerial discretion in manipulating profit. By focusing on the existence of a commitment, FRS12 should reduce the scope for this form of manipulation.

Self-insurance

It is common for companies to decide not to insure against business risks which are relatively small in the context of their own operations, preferring to bear the impact of the losses themselves. By doing so they avoid the expense of premiums, which will reflect not only the expected cost of reimbursing for losses but also administrative costs and the insurer's profit. Thus, provided that the scale of the losses in any period will not be such as seriously to damage the company, it is likely to be cheaper to follow this route. In substance, the same policy is adopted by groups of companies which include an insurance company that under-writes the losses of the rest of the group: on consolidation the group as a whole holds no external insurance. It is normal to describe this practice as 'self-insurance' but this term is misleading: although the policy may be an entirely rational one in the best interests of the shareholders, the fact remains that there is actually no insurance in place.

Until the adoption of FRS12, it had been common practice to even out the impact of losses in the profit and loss account between good years and bad, in effect charging the regular premium that would have been paid rather than the actual lumpy incidence of losses. Suppose for example that a travel company expects ten claims per annum for damages of, say, £50,000 each. It decides not to carry insurance for these and thus expects to incur a cost of £0.5 million per annum. In the first year only five claims are received and by the balance sheet date it is confident that no further claims will be received in respect of holidays the revenue for which has been included in its profit and loss account. There is no evidence that its initial estimate will prove to be wrong over time: this year has been a good year and sooner or later it can expect a bad year. Under pre-FRS12 GAAP, it could charge £0.5 million in its profit and loss account, with £250,000 representing claims already paid or owed to identified claimants and the remaining £250,000 shown as a provision.

Yet there is no obligation in respect of the latter provision: no claims will be paid out in respect of that year's trading. Under the Statement of Principles (and FRS12) profit should be £250,000 higher, showing shareholders that the company has had a good year. If it terminates its activities at that point (or takes out external insurance) the £250,000 will be available to the shareholders as profit, as shown. In the (probable) upcoming bad year, profits will be down, showing the shareholders that they have suffered a bad year. If the bad year had come before the good year, shareholders would have suffered and could not have avoided their obligations by ceasing to trade or taking out external insurance. The overall result is greater fluctuations in profit, but this will actually demonstrate to users of the financial statements the real economic consequence of the company's decision not to insure.

As the chairman of the ASB puts it:

The fact is that management is taking a risk and [under the old system] hiding that risk from users who may not want to be involved in companies that have a potential downside associated with lack of insurance. It is probably cheaper for airlines not to insure their passengers on a flight and take a chance that none of their aircraft will crash. Every flight that lands is a bonus – the company got away with it! Would shareholders, being ignorant of the lack of insurance, be happy to continue to invest in a company which, in these litigious times, could be suddenly faced with a massive legal claim even though so-called insurance premiums had passed through its accounts? (Tweedie, 1996: 30–1)

Many preparers are concerned about recording volatile profits, feeling that investors and other users prefer to see a stable situation. But however strongly users may prefer the actual situation to be stable, if it is not, there are dangers in implying, by the way it is accounted for, that it is. It is worth quoting the chairman of the ASB again:

Minimising the effects of erratic events is a job for management. To the extent volatile events occur and affect market prices we should reflect them in financial statements. Transparency is all-important – otherwise accounts will never reflect the actual risk to which investors and creditors are exposed. It is no argument in opposing a proposed standard to say that implementation might cause managers or investors to act differently. If the standard is deemed to reflect the situation appropriately, to oppose it would mean that it is better to hide reality. (Tweedie, 1996: 31)

If preparers wish to smooth out profit to the level which the entity would have earned had it taken out external insurance, they are free to make appropriations to an account within ownership interest and transter amounts back again as appropriate.

Future decommissioning costs

Decommissioning costs are the costs that arise at the end of the life of certain types of plant, such as oil rigs and nuclear power stations, where the actions necessary to terminate operations and dismantle the plant safely and lawfully can be very significant. Pre-FRS12 GAAP was to build up an amount for these costs by regular charges to the profit and loss account over the life of the plant and carrying these to a provision. To the extent that the need for the decommissioning costs comes about because of the operations of the plant, this approach still applies.

However, in many instances, a major part of the costs is caused by the fact that the plant has been constructed: even if it were not used, the costs involved in removing it would remain substantial. Under these circumstances there may well indeed be an obligation to meet decommissioning costs (the state would not permit the company simply to abandon the plant) but this obligation does not build up over the life of the plant: it is present from the point of the original commissioning. Thus FRS12 now requires decommissioning costs to be included in the cost of the asset and capitalized, provided that the other tests for capitalizing a fixed asset are met (for example, that future economic benefits will be received). The associated liability will also be included in the balance sheet. The impact on the profit and loss account will be minimal: whereas before the transfers to the provision were charged, now depreciation will be higher by the equivalent amount, reflecting the larger carrying amount capitalized.

Notes

1 Such a liability will not usually pass the appropriate recognition criteria (see Chapter 7).

2 Another case of 'hunt the past transaction or event' (see Chapter 4)?

3 Whether current GAAP classifies the amount correctly is another matter and we will return to this question in Chapter 9.

References

Davies, M., Paterson, R. and Wilson, A. (1999) *UK GAAP*, 6th edn. London: Macmillan.

Tweedie, D. (1996) 'Regulating change: the role of the conceptual statement in standard-setting', in I. Lapsley and F. Mitchell (eds), *Accounting and Performance Measurement*. London: Paul Chapman. pp. 18–34.

Further reading

For a discussion of self-insurance and restructuring provisions, see B.A. Rutherford, 'They manipulate. You smooth. I self-hedge', *Accountancy*, June 1995, p. 95.

See also the further reading for Chapter 6.

6

Elements of Financial
Statements III: Other Elements

We have now examined at length the two elements that drive the Statement of Principles' system of element definitions. The remaining elements fit into the jigsaw in exactly the way that those familiar with contemporary financial reporting would expect. The remaining element of financial position is *ownership interest* and the statement of financial position (balance sheet) is constructed according to the traditional accounting equation: ownership interest equals assets minus liabilities. The statement of financial performance (profit and loss account) is composed of *gains* and *losses*, which are defined in terms of changes in ownership interest. Finally, ownership interest can change not only as a result of gains and losses but also because the entity receives *contributions from owners* and makes *distributions to owners*.

Ownership interest

The Statement of Principles formally defines ownership interest as follows:

> Ownership interest is the residual amount found by deducting all of the entity's liabilities from all of the entity's assets. (SP, 4.37)

As the Statement points out, 'since ownership interest is defined as a residual interest, the distinction between liabilities and ownership interest is highly significant' (SP, 4.38). Furthermore, in making the distinction in practice, because ownership interest is the residual, we have only the definition of liabilities to rely on. The Statement of Principles also points out that, although owners generally invest in the hope of a return, because their interest is the residual they do not have the ability to insist on that return. In other words, they cannot insist that resources are transferred to them regardless of the circumstances. We shall see later in this chapter that this distinction is not necessarily easy to make in practice.

Two elements relate to the transactions between the entity and its owners:

Contributions from owners are increases in ownership interest resulting from transfers from owners in their capacity as owners. (SP, 4.42)

Distributions to owners are decreases in ownership interest resulting from transfers to owners in their capacity as owners. (SP, 4.42)

In both cases the transfers take place between the entity and parties who own the entity and who are dealing with the entity *as owners*. The parties concerned may also have transactions with the entity in other capacities, for example as customers, but only those transactions that follow from their ownership fall into the two categories defined above. In some cases a single transaction may combine aspects that arise from ownership and aspects that arise from other capacities and these two aspects must be distinguished from each other.

The most common case of a contribution from owners is the provision of capital, normally, in the case of a company, by the purchase of its shares. This can be either on the establishment of the company or on the issue of additional shares subsequent to its establishment. Those acquiring the shares may not have previously been owners: they become owners by virtue of the transaction. The contribution received by the company may be cash or other consideration (such as tangible assets or the performance of services) or settlement of liabilities.

Notice that someone who buys existing shares from another share-holder (for example via a stock exchange) does not undertake a trans-action with the company itself, so that no contribution from owners has to be accounted for in the financial statements of the entity when one external party buys shares from another. However, the new owner of the shares becomes an owner of the entity by virtue of acquiring the shares, so that, for example, subsequent distributions to owners will involve that party.

The most common case of a distribution to owners is the dividend paid by companies. The purchase by a company of its own shares also involves a distribution to owners: resources leave the company and there is a reduction in ownership interest because an entity cannot 'own itself'.

Financial performance

Financial performance is composed of gains and losses, which are defined as follows:

Gains are increases in ownership interest not resulting from contributions from owners. (SP, 4.39)

Losses are decreases in ownership interest not resulting from distributions to owners. (SP, 4.39)

It is important to appreciate that the Statement of Principles uses these terms in a rather different way to that in which they are employed in conventional accountancy. First, they are employed in a broad sense, to include items often referred to as revenues and expenses. Thus selling trading stock yields gains and losses in the same way as selling tangible fixed assets. Secondly, each change in assets or liabilities, considered separately, potentially gives rise to a separate gain or loss. Thus if trading stock with a carrying amount of £100 is sold for £150 we would conventionally see this as a profit of £50, but the Statement of Principles views the transaction as giving rise to a gain of £150 (the asset received) and a loss of £100 (the asset given up). It considers that 'whether such gains and losses are shown separately in the financial statements is a presentation issue' (SP, 4.41).

Perhaps surprisingly, this is all the Statement of Principles says about the elements of financial performance. Implicit in the element definitions is the adoption of what is sometimes called a *comprehensive income* approach, that is an approach under which all changes in ownership interest, other than those resulting from transactions with owners, are included in financial performance. The alternative approach is to try to discriminate between various aspects of the entity's operations. For example, it might be possible to discriminate between core and peripheral activities. Core activities would be included in financial performance, while peripheral activities, such as transactions in non-trading assets like property, would be accounted for elsewhere, perhaps as direct additions to or deductions from ownership interest in the balance sheet. Clearly, by rolling all gains into a single category, and treating all losses in the same way, the Statement of Principles is going against such an approach.

In some ways, perhaps, the Statement of Principles' brevity is inevitable given that the element definitions are so strongly derivative, but its treatment of the profit and loss account has been one of the major matters attracting criticism and we shall return to this later.

An articulating system

As we have seen (Chapter 4), because the element definitions all hinge around those of assets and liabilities, the system yields an articulating set of financial statements:

1   Whenever an asset is recognized, there must also be recognized, to an equal amount, either liabilities, or reductions in other assets, or changes in ownership interest, or a combination of these.

2   Whenever a liability is recognized, there must also be recognized, to an equal amount, either assets, or reductions in other liabilities, or changes in ownership interest, or a combination of these.
3   Whenever contributions from, or distributions to, owners are recognized, there must also be recognized a combination of assets and liabilities to an equal amount.
4   Whenever gains or losses are recognized, ownership interest will change by an equal amount (since gains and losses are defined in these terms).

In this way (at least), the Statement's system of element definitions corresponds to the orthodox approach to the financial statements.

Criticisms of the ASB's approach

Matching

The matching principle occupies a position at the core of contemporary accounting practice. According to SSAP2,

> revenues and costs are accrued (that is, recognised as they are earned or incurred, not as money is received or paid), matched with one another so far as their relationship can be established or justifiably assumed, and dealt with in the profit and loss account of the period to which they relate. (paragraph 14(b))

This is reinforced by company law (CA, Schedule 4).

The name 'matching' was coined by W.A. Paton and A.C. Littleton in a 1940 US monograph which offered a rationale for the current practice of the time which many regarded as markedly better developed than anything that had been achieved before. Under the matching concept, periodic income determination (that is, measuring income for a given period) occupies the primary role in financial accounting. Assets are viewed as deferred expenses, that is, costs already incurred which will be matched with income in future periods. This approach to the definition of assets is embodied in the following description of current practice:

> A non-monetary asset in a historical cost system is purely a deferred cost, a cost which has been incurred before the balance sheet date and, on an accruals basis, is expected (with sufficient certainty to jump the prudence hurdle) to benefit periods beyond the balance sheet date, so as to justify its being carried forward. This general description fits every non-monetary asset in the historical cost balance sheet, whether it be stock, repayments, tangible fixed assets, deferred development expenditure or whatever. (Paterson, 1988: 26)

The matching concept, in its strongest form, clearly gives primacy to the determination of gains and losses (periodic income determination) and makes assets and liabilities the derivative concepts. If a cost has been incurred and, under the matching rules, it is appropriate to charge that cost against income in a future period, it is an asset up to that point. Equally, if a cost can be matched with income in the current period but no obligation has yet been settled, a liability arises in the balance sheet at the end of the period whether or not an obligation to a third party can be identified, and that liability remains until an obligation is settled.

It is important to emphasize that the treatment of most items is the same under both a matching-driven approach and the Statement of Principles. However, a matching-driven system can treat certain items in ways which differ from treatment they receive under the Statement of Principles:

1   Some items which do not qualify as assets under the Statement of Principles, because they do not represent future economic benefits, can be treated as assets because they are costs which have been incurred and which the entity intends to match against future profits. Examples (see Chapter 4) include: (a) operating costs of unused capacity on start-up; and (b) deferred operating expenditure.
2   Some items which do not qualify as liabilities under the Statement of Principles, because they do not represent current obligations, can be treated as liabilities because they are costs which will be incurred and which the entity wishes to match against current profits. Examples (see Chapter 5) include: (a) long-term infrastructural maintenance where there is no actual deterioration in the asset; (b) business restructuring costs; and (c) proposed dividends.
3   Items that are charged in the profit and loss account in the same year under both the Statement of Principles and matching can be classified differently in the balance sheet. Examples (see Chapter 5) include: (a) long-term infrastructural maintenance where there is an actual deterioration in the asset; and (b) future decommissioning costs.

Those who defend the matching approach argue that the treatments under this approach set out above are appropriate and that, without them, assets and liabilities are misstated and periodic income is distorted. Some commentators on the Statement of Principles have advanced this position very strongly:

> The Statement of Principles' principles are . . . a decisive break with the past. The pre-eminence previously ascribed to matching . . . is formally abandoned, and the effect will be to undermine financial reporting . . . In a going concern,

business activity is a continuum without a natural beginning or end. Accounting periods are arbitrary. Furthermore, the income-earning cycles, ranging
from days (retail) to decades (energy and extractive industries), are unrelated
to the solar year. The Statement of Principles' emphasis on year-end balance
sheet values is inconsistent with this reality. The annual accounting cycle is
merely a convenience for investors and tax collectors – a fact inherent in the
matching concept but seriously underestimated in the Statement of Principles
. . . Revenue, expenses and profit, not the entity's resources and their use, are
the lifeblood of business . . . The allocation of historical cost transactions to
arbitrary accounting periods, not assets and liabilities, is the essence of
accounting. (Davies and Davies, 1999: 83)

Our more general concern is that we simply do not think the ASB's approach
works well in practice, because it starts from the wrong place. It implies that
accounts are drawn up through a disconnected process of recognising and
measuring assets and liabilities in the balance sheet. In reality, of course,
accounts are prepared from the company's accounting records, and by
allocating transactions to the accounting periods to which they belong, and it is
this process of allocation that creates balances that end up in the balance sheet.
This is the basis of the fundamental accounting concepts set out in SSAP2 and
the Companies Act, notably the accruals [i.e. matching] and prudence
concepts. (Ernst and Young, 1996: 13)

Why, then, does the Statement of Principles seek to move practice away
from the strong-form matching approach? We can examine reasons
under two categories, though they are interrelated. The first category
covers theoretical arguments.

Let us remind ourselves that the conceptual framework of the Statement of Principles seeks to provide rigorously developed fundamental
terms from which accounting rules can be derived: this is its purpose if it
is to be of help in devising accounting standards. If it is to succeed, the
fundamental terms it contains must not be derived from, or include
reference to, accounting rules, otherwise the structure becomes circular:
we would be deriving fundamental terms from accounting rules and
then deriving accounting rules from the fundamental terms. The definitions of assets and liabilities satisfy this requirement. If matching is to
replace these at the heart of the system it would be necessary to have
either a definition of matching, or, what would amount to much the
same thing, definitions of gains and losses, that were rigorous, independent of accounting rules, and not derived from the definitions of
assets and liabilities.

The problem for those who defend the matching concept is that no
such definitions exist (SP, Appendix III, paragraph 29). The explanation
of matching set out in SSAP2 (quoted above) talks of recognizing
revenues and costs 'as they are earned or incurred' and matching them
'so far as their relationship can be established or justifiably assumed'. But
how do we tell when they have been earned or incurred and what
constitutes a justifiable assumption of a relationship? The only answers

we can infer from practice are that revenues and costs are earned or incurred when the accounting rules say they are incurred or earned and that a justifiable assumption is one that is contained in the accounting rules.

Thus the matching concept becomes just a roundabout way of saying that accountants do what accountants do. It has been argued that matching is essentially a metaphor, attractive to the accounting profession because it is so vivid, but flawed because it masks significant differences between the image employed and the object being described (see, for example, Thompson, 1991). Paton himself expressed regret at the role his monograph had played in promoting what he referred to as the matching 'gospel' (Thompson, 1991: 88).

Attempts to construct definitions of assets and liabilities that incorporate the strong-form matching approach reflect the circularity referred to above. A classic definition under this approach is the following:

> Assets: economic resources of an enterprise that are recognised and measured in conformity with generally accepted accounting principles. Assets also include certain deferred charges that are not resources but that are recognised and measured in conformity with generally accepted accounting principles. (Accounting Principles Board, 1970, paragraph 132)

The second sentence undermines the reference to economic resources in the first and effectively allows into the definition anything that is currently treated as an asset by accountants as a group, that is, provided that an individual accountant is following generally accepted accounting principles.

A conceptual framework that was built on the matching concept would thus lack rigour and would describe current practice rather than providing a means of improving it. As Robert Sprouse put it, 'the matching concept may be deemed to supply adequate support for virtually any accounting procedure' (1971: 94). It certainly supports, for example, both the pre-SSAP21 treatment of leased assets and the SSAP21 treatment and both the capitalization and the immediate write-off of development expenditure and goodwill. There would thus be little value in such an approach from the point of view of standard-setters looking for guidance on discriminating between good and bad practice. Those who criticize the Statement of Principles on the grounds that it departs from strong-form matching are effectively arguing that standard-setters should not employ a conceptual framework at all, but rather make pragmatic adjustments to current practice on the basis of individual considerations specific to the topic under consideration.

The second category of arguments against matching is more pragmatic (see Tweedie, 1996: 31–2). If something being carried on the balance sheet as an asset does not in fact reflect future economic benefits but is merely the consequence of accounting procedures, is the resulting balance sheet a faithful reflection of underlying reality? If users discover that there are no future economic benefits embodied in the balance sheet item, are they likely to consider the accounting treatment acceptable? If the business founders and is discovered to have on its balance sheet substantial carrying amounts attributable to such assets, will users consider that financial statements, and the accountants who prepared them, are useful?

It might be thought that, on this argument, permitting liabilities to be recognized 'in advance' of actual obligations should be encouraged as prudent. But by permitting entities to recognize liabilities under these circumstances, accounting rules effectively allow managers discretion to make charges to the profit and loss account at a time of their choosing and, perhaps, to make credits at their discretion too, by 'releasing' provisions made in earlier periods and subsequently found to be unnecessary. This amounts to income smoothing and, while it may make the balance sheet prudent (in the traditional sense of the term), renders the profit and loss account unreliable.

A further defence of the abandonment of strong-form matching, offered by the Statement of Principles (SP, Appendix III, paragraph 29), is that all the other conceptual frameworks developed by comparable countries, and by the IASC, do the same thing. While not a powerful defence in theoretical terms, it should perhaps be seen as underlining the importance of the other arguments set out here.

One consequence of the move from matching to the Statement of Principles' approach may be that profit becomes a more volatile accounting number. This is because strong-form matching permits accountants to spread amounts across several accounting periods and thereby smooth out the stream of profit numbers (see, for example, the treatment of operating costs of unused capacity on start-up in Chapter 4) or to charge equal amounts rather than fluctuating amounts period by period (see, for example, the treatment of self-insurance in Chapter 5). But if the underlying position being reported is volatile, surely the accounting numbers should reflect this, rather than being smoothed out to mask the underlying reality from users?

One criticism that is sometimes made of the Statement of Principles' system of definitions is that it implies that the profit and loss account itself is somehow being downgraded. This does not, however, strictly follow from the stance on element definitions and the ASB has gone to some length to explain that it is not seeking to diminish the status of the profit and loss account (see, for example, SP, Appendix III, paragraph 39).

Though the Statement of Principles rejects the use of the matching concept in its strongest form, it does employ matching in addressing questions such as how to allocate the cost of fixed assets, essentially a recognition issue to be discussed in the following chapter.

Definitions are derivative

It is not, in itself, a criticism of the system of element definitions to say that the rest of the system is derived from the definition of assets. We do, however, need to recognize the consequences of this feature of the system. The articulation of the statements of financial performance and financial position results from the derivative nature of the elements of the statement of financial performance and not from any characteristic of the relationship between the underlying 'real-world' concepts of (a) gains and losses and (b) assets and liabilities. Indeed, the concepts of gains and losses are not separate from those of assets and liabilities, any more than the concepts of getting taller and ageing are separate from the concepts of height and age.

Let us examine this idea a little further. Assets and liabilities exist independently of the methods accountants use to recognize and measure them and the Statement of Principles deals with each stage of the process in turn, asking first, does this item satisfy the definition of an asset or liability; then, if it does satisfy the definition, should it be recognized; and finally, if it should be recognized, how should it be measured?

Gains and losses are changes in ownership interest, which in turn is changes in assets less liabilities. The identification of changes necessarily involves recognition and measurement. This clearly applies when a gain or loss derives from remeasuring the same asset or liability. What happens when assets and liabilities are exchanged, as when stock is purchased or sold?

Let us first consider the case of an exchange, such as a sale of stock, which under conventional accountancy would enter into income determination. Assume for convenience the sale is made for cash. Let us take it that stock with a cost of £100 is sold for £150. The Statement of Principles regards the reduction in one asset (stock) as yielding a gross loss of £100 and the increase in the other (cash) as yielding a gross gain of £150, with the decision about whether or not to set one against the other to show a net gain or loss as a matter of mere presentation. In a conventional profit and loss account the gross gain is shown as sales and the gross loss as cost of sales. The gross gain and loss involved are a function of, among other things, the recognition and measurement of the assets in the exchange.

Now consider the purchase of stock. Again, for convenience let us assume the purchase is made for cash. Let us take it that stock costing £80 is purchased. Conventional accountancy would see this as an exchange which does not enter into income determination, so that it is regarded as yielding neither a gain nor a loss, and thus would not be reflected in the statement of financial performance. The profit and loss account of an entity which entered into both the sale of stock discussed in the previous paragraph and the purchase of stock discussed here would thus include only the following:

	£
Gains:	
Sales	<u>150</u>
Losses:	
Cost of sales	<u>100</u>
Overall result	<u>50</u>

The purchase of stock would not feature in the statement.

It is not clear whether the Statement of Principles would take the same view (so that the numbers in the statement of financial performance would be as above), or whether it would regard the acquisition of the stock as a gross gain of £80 and the reduction in cash of £80 as a gross loss. If the gain and loss are taken to be equal, the overall impact on financial performance will be the same under both approaches. Under the latter approach, it would be possible to show the gain and loss separately (though the statement of financial performance would then look rather unlike a conventional profit and loss account) or net the two against each other. If the gain and loss are shown separately, the statement of financial performance would look like this:

	£
Gains:	
Sales	150
Acquisition of stock	<u>80</u>
	<u>230</u>
Losses:	
Cost of sales	100
Consideration for stock	<u>80</u>
	<u>180</u>
Overall result	<u>50</u>

If the gain and loss are netted against each other, the statement of financial performance would look like this:

	£	£
Purchases of stock:		
Gains	80	
Losses	<u>80</u>	
Net result		nil
Sales:		
Gains – sales	150	
Losses – cost of sales	<u>100</u>	
Net result		<u>50</u>
Overall result		<u>50</u>

Now, if the purchase transaction is excluded from the statement of financial performance, or is placed in a separate section, some rationale has to be found for distinguishing this transaction from a sale. We cannot say we are distinguishing it because it yields neither a net profit nor a net loss, because to do so would also exclude from the statement of financial performance those sales that break even. Thus we must be excluding it because we have determined in advance that it will yield neither a profit nor a loss: in other words we have decided not to recognize a profit or loss at this point. This, in turn, means that the *structure* of the statement of financial performance – which transactions will be included in the statement and which will be excluded, or which will be netted off – is itself derived from not only the *definitions* of assets and liabilities but also the *recognition* of assets and liabilities. Even if the gross gains and losses on purchase transactions are included in the general categories of gains and losses (the first of the two presentations above), the recognition of gains and losses is clearly derived from of the recognition of assets and liabilities.

In all cases, the determination of gains and losses has involved consideration not only of whether assets and liabilities exist but also of their recognition and measurement. Thus our concepts of gains and losses are derived from not only the definitions of assets and liabilities but also the recognition and measurement methods applied to them.

Components of comprehensive income

A number of commentators have criticized the Statement of Principles' use of the comprehensive income approach. The chapter of the Statement dealing with presentation (see Chapter 9 of this book) makes some comments on how gains and losses should be presented in the statement of financial performance. These critics would prefer that the importance of distinguishing between gains and losses that are central to the entity's operations, recurrent and subject to management control (or, at least, influence), and those that are peripheral, unlikely to recur or outside management control, should be recognized by including some form of distinction in the system of element definitions, as is the case in, for example, the US conceptual framework.

Other criticisms

The Statement provides no element definitions for items that appear in the cash flow statement, arguing that 'analysis into elements is not relevant to that statement' (SP, 4.4). Not all commentators would agree with that position: some would hold that cash inflows and outflows, for example, could be element definitions in the same way as gains and losses.

A further criticism concerns the effectiveness of the approach in distinguishing debt and equity. We shall see examples of this problem in examining applications of the definitions in the next section.

Applications

Capital instruments

Capital instruments are the instruments issued by an entity as a means of raising finance, including shares, debentures, loans and debt instruments, options and warrants that give holders the right to subscribe for or obtain capital instruments (see FRS4). According to the Statement of Principles, all capital instruments must constitute either liabilities, if there is an obligation, or ownership interest:

> owners, unlike creditors, do not have the ability to insist that a transfer is made to them regardless of the circumstances: theirs is a residual interest in the assets of the entity after all liabilities have been deducted. (SP, 4.38)

This definition of ownership interest clearly applies to ordinary share capital, and could also be argued to apply to preference share capital because preference shareholders cannot insist on their fixed rate dividends if there is no profit out of which to pay them and, on a liquidation, have no right to participate in the assets of the company if there are no assets left after repaying creditors. It will also apply to the minority interests in subsidiaries, to the same extent that it applies to the capital instruments owned by majority owners.

In practice, preference shares may come close to being liabilities. This is especially true where: (a) the dividend rights are cumulative, as is commonly the case (that is, even if there is insufficient profit in one year to pay a dividend, that dividend is paid together with subsequent years' dividends, if profits from subsequent years become available); and (b) the shares are redeemable, the redemption date is in the reasonably foreseeable future and there appears to be little prospect of the company suffering serious financial difficulty in the meantime.

Further, increasingly complex capital instruments are being issued and it is not easy to see how the definition of a liability resolves the question of whether they are ownership interest or a liability. As an example, consider the case of a zero coupon bond, issued today at £65 and convertible at £100 in five years' time to ordinary shares. It might be argued that in commercial effect this instrument is debt for the first five years, bearing interest at a rate which compounds the principal of £65 to a value of £100 over the period, and this is how it should be accounted for under FRS4. Thereafter it is converted to ownership interest. However, in the first five years of its life there is no obligation to pay interest and there is no obligation to settle a liability by transfer of resources in five years' time, only an obligation to issue ordinary shares. Some commentators would argue that the question of how the instrument should be dealt with in the first five years of its life, as debt or equity, is not resolved by the Statement of Principles. Others would argue that, if the arrangement is in substance borrowing, there is an obligation to pay (implicit) interest and to redeem capital, settled after five years by the issue of equity instruments.

Deferred tax

Historically, it was customary to account for tax under what is now called the *flow-through* method. The charge for tax in the profit and loss account for a period represented the tax falling due in respect of the taxable profit for that period, and the tax liability in the balance sheet represented the cumulative amount of these sums less amounts actually paid.

Taxable profit differs from the profit recognized in the profit and loss account for a variety of reasons and governments sometimes allow very substantial differences between the two, for example to influence the behaviour of companies. An example was the system of '100% first year allowances' under which companies were allowed to set the full cost of some types of capital expenditure against taxable profit in the year in which the expenditure was incurred as an incentive to expand investment programmes. The cost of the capital expenditure would be reflected in the calculation of profit via the depreciation charge and would thus extend over a number of periods. As a result, taxable profit would be much lower than accounting profit in a year of heavy capital expenditure and hence the tax charge would be relatively low. This effect is reversed in future years as the annual depreciation charge continues to affect accounting profit but is not allowable against taxable profit, which can thus exceed accounting profit. However, if the business is expanding, or prices are rising, the increasing capital expenditure in future years generates further first year allowances and the effect could be to postpone actual payments to the tax authorities for a number of periods, if not indefinitely.

Unless the effect is genuinely to postpone the payment of the tax indefinitely, the result of the flow-through method is that the total tax that will be paid by an entity as a result of the accounting profits it earns in a given period falls into a number of periods, stretching forward from the point at which the capital expenditure is incurred. It can be argued that, under these circumstances, users may be misled as to the amount of tax that the entity will have to meet as a result of the profits it is including in its financial statements. Accounting practice developed a means of responding to this problem by recording *deferred tax*, which can be thought of as reflecting timing differences between the recognition of accounting profit and the impact of taxation. Such an approach, currently required by SSAP15, can easily be justified as matching costs (taxation) and revenues.

The question, however, is: does deferred tax satisfy the definition of a liability under the Statement of Principles?[1] There is no legal liability, as at the balance sheet date, to make a payment to the tax authorities. Is there a constructive obligation? One way of approaching this question is to see whether settlement occurs. If the impact of the transactions which are reducing tax (in the example considered above, the capital expenditure) is short-lived, actual cash payments will be made to the tax authorities within the foreseeable future. But suppose the transactions go on occurring, with the result that actual cash payments continue to be low or non-existent indefinitely? In each accounting period it is possible to distinguish two effects:

1   the amount by which taxable profit exceeds accounting profit as a result of the reversal of timing differences originating in previous periods – and thus the amount of additional tax that would fall due as a result of this
2   the amount by which taxable profit falls below accounting profit as a result of new transactions, that is, timing differences originating in the period – and thus the amount by which tax is reduced as a result.

The deferred tax balance can be justified as a liability on the argument that, at any point in time, future tax assessments will be higher than they would have been, had taxable and accounting profit been fully aligned, and those increments in future tax assessments constitute a constructive obligation. In other words, the amount described at 1 above should have been included in earlier balance sheets as a liability (just like amounts to be paid to suppliers in a period as a result of the acquisition of stock in earlier periods), even though it may not actually be settled in cash because it will be offset by the new originating timing differences described at 2. The amounts are, on this argument, settled by offset against the new originating differences, which would, indeed, have reduced tax still further had it not been for the reversal of the earlier timing differences. In the words of the ASB:

Those who see . . . deferred tax . . . as . . . [a] liability do so on the grounds that, at any point in the life of the [capital equipment], the . . . entity's tax assessments for future periods will, as a result of the capital allowances claimed in the current and previous periods, be higher . . . than they would have been if there had been a different pattern of allowances claimed. Accordingly, where there is a difference between depreciation and capital allowances claimed, the future cash flows relating to tax assessments will be different from those that would have arisen if capital allowances claimed had equalled depreciation charged. (DP, *Accounting for Tax*, paragraph 4.4.10)

Some commentators, however, take a different view:

> On a strict reading of the framework, deferred tax would be abolished and therefore no attempt would be made to match tax with the accounting profit that it relates to. This is because deferred tax does not meet the definition of a liability under the framework. (The ASB's discussion paper on tax does attempt to rationalise it as a liability, but implausibly in our view.) (Ernst and Young, 1996: 8)

The main argument offered by those who advance this position is that the rationale set out above depends on a hypothetical alternative position: tax would have been different if the tax regime had been different. Settlement of the putative liability occurs when the hypothetical difference reverses, rather than when an actual payment is made to a third party. But *any* alternative hypothetical position could be assumed, so the issue becomes: what is special about the particular hypothetical position that the profile of deductions made from accounting and taxable profit are identical? The plausibility of this particular hypothetical position seems to be linked back to matching: to a desire to bring accounting and taxable profit into line, period by period.

We need not attempt to resolve here the question of whether deferred tax is a liability: the problem serves to underline the complexities of applying a conceptual framework in practice.

Hedges of uncontracted future transactions

Hedging is a feature of the financial management of businesses which involves acquiring financial instruments with the intention of reducing the risk associated with some aspect of the businesses' mainstream operations. The financial instrument acquired is referred to as the *hedge* and the aspect of operations generating the risk that the hedge is designed to reduce is referred to as the *hedged position*.

Normally, unless financial instruments are a hedge, they will be accounted for separately according to their own characteristics. Suppose, for example, a company operating in the UK enters into a contract to sell $100,000 in the following accounting period at $2.00 per £1.00, at a time when the current exchange rate is $2.00 per £1.00. At the time of entering into the contract, it has no value because it simply represents an opportunity to undertake a transaction yielding neither gain nor loss, namely to trade pounds for dollars at the current exchange rate. Now suppose that, by the end of the current accounting period, the rate of exchange is $3.00 per £1.00. The contract now represents a valuable opportunity: its owner can purchase $100,000 in the open market for £33,333 and sell them to the counterparty to the contract for £50,000. Because the contract represents a valuable opportunity, the company owning it will be able to sell it for its value, in this case the profit on the transaction of £16,667. If the instrument is recorded in the balance sheet at fair value, the company will recognize a profit in the current accounting year of £16,667 and an increase in its assets of the same amount, representing the increase in the fair value of the instrument from nil at the time of purchase. If the company actually disposes of the instrument by the end of the accounting period it will certainly record the profit of £16,667.

However, if the instrument in question had been acquired as a hedge, current accounting practice would reflect the transactions rather differently. Suppose that the company expects to make sales, in the following accounting period, amounting to $100,000. At the current exchange rate of $2.00 per £1.00 it expects to receive foreign exchange that it can convert into pounds to the value of £50,000. The goods will be manufactured in the UK so that the cost of sales associated with the dollar sales will be incurred in pounds. The amount involved is £40,000, so that the company expects to show a profit of £10,000 on the relevant sales. It is, however, concerned that the exchange rate may move against it and cause a deterioration in the value of the sales in pounds and hence its profit. In order to reduce this risk it enters into the contract described above as a hedge against movements in the dollar.

By the end of the accounting period in which the instrument is purchased, the exchange rate has moved, as before, to $3.00 per £1.00. Remember that the sales will occur in the following accounting period. The impact of those sales on the profit and loss account of the company (which is measured in pounds) will now be as follows:

	£
Sales – $100,000 at $3.00 per £1.00	33,333
Cost of sales	40,000
Loss	(6,667)

This is the loss the hedge was designed to prevent. Current accounting practice for hedging reflects the intention behind the hedge by deferring recognition of the gain on the hedge until the hedged position unwinds. Thus no gain is recognized in the first accounting period (because the sales have yet to be made) and the profit and loss account in the second period records both the result of the sales (as above) and the gain on the hedge (£16,667) – a net result of £10,000 profit, which is the sum that was expected when the exchange rate stood at $2.00 per £1.00.

Current hedge accounting practice thus permits the profit and loss account to record what management intended to occur when it acquired the hedge (assuming everything else works out as expected). It requires, however, either (a) that the gain on the hedge in the first period and the entity's ownership of a valuable instrument at the end of the first period be omitted completely from the financial statements; or (b) that the instrument be included in the balance sheet but the accompanying credit entry be treated not as a gain but as a liability.

Now you may feel that omitting a gain on a financial instrument yet to be sold, or treating it as a liability, is not too serious, but remember two things. First, the exchange rate could have moved the other way. The hedge is still effective, in the sense that when the sales are made the dollars bring in more pounds than expected, but the loss on the forward purchase of pounds brings the net result back to the expected amount. However, deferring recognition of the loss involves either omitting it from the financial statements of the first period altogether or treating it as an asset. Secondly, hedge accounting as currently practised permits the gain or loss to be omitted from the profit and loss account in the first period even when the instrument has been disposed of, so that a gain would normally be regarded as realized even under historical cost accounting.

The only way round this problem is to include the gain or loss in the first period in a special section of the profit and loss account and then bring it back into the main profit and loss account in the second period to offset the result of the unwinding of the hedged position (this is sometimes called *recycling*).

The pressure to permit hedge accounting here results from a combination of a historical commitment to strong-form matching and a view that accounting should reflect the purpose of the actual transactions being entered into, namely hedging the business's exposure to the risks to its future income and cash flows. However, as the ASB admits,

> if hedge accounting is used for hedges of uncontracted future transactions, there is an uncomfortable choice of whether it is better to do violence to the balance sheet [by including a gain or loss as if it were an asset or liability] or to [comprehensive income, as a result of recycling]. In principle, it seems that the 'right answer' is not to allow hedge accounting for hedges of future transactions. (DP, *Derivatives and Other Financial Instruments*, paragraph 4.5.3)

The way in which hedges of uncontracted future transactions are treated by standard-setting bodies will be an important test of their conceptual frameworks.

Notes

1 Timing differences may in practice yield a debit balance on deferred tax, so that the question becomes: does it satisfy the definition of an asset? Such circumstances are not considered here.

References

Accounting Principles Board (1970) *Statement 4: Basic Concepts and Accounting Principles*. New York: Accounting Principles Board.

Davies, M. and Davies, P. (1999) 'The ASB has got it wrong', *Accountancy*, June: 83.

Ernst and Young (1996) *The ASB's Framework: Time to Decide*. London: Ernst & Young.

Paterson, R. (1988) 'Building the right framework', *Accountancy*, October: 26–7.

Paton, W.A. and Littleton, A.C. (1940) *An Introduction to Corporate Accounting Standards*. Evanston, IL: American Accounting Association.

Sprouse, R.T. (1971) 'The balance sheet – embodiment of the most fundamental elements of accounting theory', in W.E. Stone (ed.), *Foundations of Accounting Theory*. Gainesville, FL: University of Florida Press.

Thompson, G.D. (1991) 'The Paton and Littleton monograph: landmark or folly?', *Accounting History* (Australia), 80–93.

Tweedie, D. (1996) 'Regulating change: the role of the conceptual statement in standard-setting', in I. Lapsley and F. Mitchell (eds), *Accounting and Performance Measurement*. London: Paul Chapman. pp. 18–34.

Further reading

For a discussion of the rationale for treating deferred tax as a liability, see DP *Accounting for Tax*, 4.4.

For a discussion of the problems of accounting for hedges of uncontracted future transactions, see DP *Derivatives and Other Financial Instruments*, Chapter 4.

For a defence of traditional accounting concepts, see M. Davies and P. Davies, 'The ASB has got it wrong', *Accountancy*, June 1999, p. 83; Ernst and Young, *The ASB's Framework: Time to Decide*, London: Ernst and Young, 1996; and R. Paterson, 'Building the right framework', *Accountancy*, October 1988, pp. 26–7.

For an explanation of the ASB's reasons for adopting its system of element definitions, see D. Tweedie, 'Regulating change: the role of the conceptual statement in standard-setting', in I. Lapsley and F. Mitchell (eds), *Accounting and Performance Measurement*. London: Paul Chapman, 1996, pp. 18–34.

For further discussion of the derivative nature of the definitions of elements of the financial performance statement, see B.A. Rutherford, 'A note on the definitions of expense used in certain conceptual frameworks', *British Accounting Review*, 1991, pp. 235–41.

7

Recognition

In simple terms, *recognizing* an item means including it in the financial statements. We have already seen that, under the Statement of Principles, no item should be included in the financial statements unless it satisfies the definition of an element of the financial statements. This principle plays an important part in delimiting what can and what cannot be done in financial reporting and thus in providing a rigorous rationale for the process. In addition to this requirement, the Statement of Principles provides a set of criteria to determine whether or not an item which satisfies the definition of an element should be recognized.

In view of the way in which element definitions are arrived at, you might think that it would be desirable for *all* items satisfying the definitions to be included in the financial statements. After all, users wanting to evaluate an entity's ability to generate earnings and cash will surely be interested in all the future economic benefits to which it controls access at a given moment (that is, all its assets) and all its obligations to transfer such benefits to other parties (that is, all its liabilities). Users are, indeed, likely to be interested in all the entity's assets and liabilities: put another way, information about all assets and liabilities will be relevant to users. The key to understanding the need for recognition criteria is the qualitative characteristics of financial information developed in Chapter 3 and, in particular, the need for information to be reliable as well as relevant. The recognition criteria are designed to ensure that information included in the financial statements passes the test of reliability as well as being relevant. The principal reason for lack of reliability is the inevitable uncertainty attaching to financial statement elements.

The element definitions and the recognition criteria provide a very powerful method of analysing whether or not individual items should be recognized in the financial statements. The way in which the two tests combine together also helps to explain why accountants behave as they do: indeed many passages in the history of standard-setting can be seen as a search for balance between relevance (implying the need to show as many as possible of the items qualifying as elements) and reliability (with the need for caution about how far to go). One example here is the case of research and development expenditure, discussed later in this chapter.

The nature of recognition

The conceptual framework defines recognition as follows:

> The term 'recognised' is used in the Statement to mean depicting an item both in words and by a monetary amount and including that amount in the primary financial statement totals. (SP, p. 59)

This apparently rather elaborate description is useful in distinguishing formal recognition in the financial statements proper from vaguer and less formal ways of disclosure, such as inclusion in other statements that do not articulate with the primary statements or in a note to the primary financial statements.

The definition emphasizes that recognition means more than disclosure, no matter where in the accounts the disclosure takes place: the accounting number established by recognizing the item must also be counted in determining gains and losses or net assets. It follows from this that even including a number on the face of the primary financial statement will not qualify as recognition if it is done in a way that excludes the figures from the totals of the statement. On the other hand, an item which is included in a group of similar items and shown in the primary financial statements in aggregate is nonetheless recognized in those statements: it may or may not also be shown separately in a note, for example in a breakdown of the aggregate total, but this does not affect its status as having been recognized in the primary financial statements.

The recognition process is not the last stage in determining the content and presentation of the primary financial statements. Elements have to be *measured* and this is the subject of the next chapter. Finally, the presentation of the statements for entities of any realistic degree of complexity will involve a process of *classification and aggregation*. This process should not affect the financial statement totals (which are determined only by recognition criteria and measurement methods), but will influence how the elements are displayed and thus the amount of information users can obtain from the statements. This process is discussed in Chapter 9.

Much of the Statement of Principles' examination of recognition is concerned with only two of the financial statement elements, assets and liabilities. This is scarcely surprising since, as pointed out in Chapter 6, the framework's system of definitions revolves around these two elements, with all other definitions being in some way derived from this pair. This in turn means that the process of recognition focuses on the balance sheet. This is a logically valid move (though, as we have seen, not one that has satisfied all commentators on the Statement of Principles) because the interlocking nature of the system of definitions means that, by recognizing assets and liabilities, we automatically take care of the consequences for the recognition of the other elements.

The recognition process

The recognition process falls into three stages:

1 Initial recognition, that is the incorporation of an element into the financial statements for the first time.
2 Subsequent remeasurement, that is changing the amount at which a previously recognized item is stated. This stage does not necessarily imply changing the measurement method but usually represents an adjustment within the measurement method under use.
3 Derecognition, that is removing from the financial statements a previously recognized item.

The recognition process involves scrutinizing the transactions and other events that may have had an effect on an entity's assets and liabilities and, as far as possible, identifying those effects and reflecting them in the financial statements in an appropriate manner. The most common form of events that require scrutiny is the transactions into which the entity has entered and, indeed, accounting is often described as 'transactions based'. However, other events may also result in recognition or derecognition of items. Examples include the invention of a new product, processing work in progress, the imposition of a fine, a fire damaging an entity's property, plant and equipment, and the passage of time.

The interrelationship between the elements of financial statements means that recognizing an element, or a change in an element (including derecognizing an element), inevitably involves recognizing another element or change in an element. Thus, for example, if a new asset is recognized, there will also be recognized some combination of: (a) a new or increased liability; (b) a decrease in another asset; (c) a gain; and (d) a contribution from owners.

A transaction or other event can impact on the recognition process in a number of ways:

1 It might yield items that satisfy the definitions of assets or liabilities and must thus be scrutinized to see whether they satisfy the relevant recognition criteria.
2 It might provide additional evidence about assets or liabilities already in existence which have hitherto not been recognized because until now they have not satisfied the relevant recognition criteria.
3 It might change aspects of assets and liabilities that have already been recognized, including the nature of the item (for example, when work in progress becomes finished goods) or the flow of benefits associated with it (for example, when a hitherto sound debt goes bad as a result of the debtor's insolvency).

4   It might involve transferring or consuming part or all of the economic benefits embodied in a previously recognized asset or settling part or all of the obligations embodied in a previously recognized liability.

Recognition criteria

The recognition criteria established by the Statement of Principles follow directly from the objective and qualitative characteristics of financial information established earlier. Thus the recognition criteria are the embodiment of the framework's concern to provide useful information for assessing stewardship and making economic decisions and, in doing so, to achieve relevance and reliability. There are different criteria for each stage in the recognition process and we will see how each set of criteria relates to the objective and qualitative characteristics of financial information as we come to them.

Initial recognition

According to the Statement of Principles:

> If a transaction or other event has created a new asset or liability or added to an existing asset or liability, that effect will be recognised if:
>
> (a)   sufficient evidence exists that the new asset or liability has been created or that there has been an addition to an existing asset or liability; and
> (b)   the new asset or liability or the addition to the existing asset or liability can be measured at a monetary amount with sufficient reliability. (SP, p. 59)

The link between criterion (a) and the objective of financial statements is as follows. The definitions of assets and liabilities are themselves derived from the objective of financial statements, so that the reporting of items satisfying the definitions will yield information contributing to this objective. Information about assets and liabilities will provide information about financial position, performance and adaptability, of use in assessing stewardship and making economic decisions. Thus this information will meet the qualitative characteristic of relevance. Hence the criterion is designed in part to establish that the items reported do indeed satisfy the definitions and are thus relevant.

The opening phrase in criterion (a) ('sufficient evidence exists') also addresses the qualitative characteristic of reliability. Only if there is sufficient evidence of the change can an asset or liability be reliably reported. This evidence responds to uncertainty as to whether an asset or liability exists and the Statement of Principles calls this *element uncertainty* (SP, 5.12). The evidence must be sufficient in both quantity and quality but the uncertainty inherent in the nature of assets and liabilities means that it cannot be expected to be conclusive. Sources of evidence will include: (a) the transaction or other event itself; (b) similar transactions or events; (c) current information relating to the possible asset or liability; and (d) similar transactions by other entities.

Criterion (b) also addresses the issue of reliability by requiring that as well as sufficient evidence, there must be a way of measuring the element with sufficient reliability and, since it is needed under the definition of recognition, the measurement must be at a monetary amount. This criterion responds to what the Statement of Principles calls *measurement uncertainty*. Measurement is dealt with in the next chapter.[1]

Subsequent remeasurement

This stage in the recognition process is discussed by the Statement of Principles as part of its coverage of measurement and will be dealt with in Chapter 8.

Derecognition

The Statement of Principles indicates that:

> An asset or liability will be wholly or partly derecognised if:
>
> (a)   sufficient evidence exists that a transaction or other past event has eliminated all or part of a previously recognised asset or liability; or
> (b)   although the item continues to be an asset or liability, the criteria for recognition are no longer met. (SP, pp. 59–60)

The term *eliminated* is used here to embrace the consumption, transfer, disposal and expiry of assets and the transfer, expiry and extinguishment of liabilities.

Derecognition when a previously recognized asset has been eliminated is normally fairly straightforward. Thus, for example, cash is 'derecognized' when it is paid out by the entity (transferred), raw materials in stock are derecognized as they are transformed into work in progress (consumed), and so on. Problems arise when some of the future economic benefits embodied in a previously recognized asset or some of the obligations embodied in a previously recognized liability are eliminated but others remain. Apart from the case of depreciation, this used to be an infrequent occurrence but more sophisticated approaches to business, and especially developments such as financial engineering, have made it increasingly common for assets and liabilities to be 'unbundled' in this way.

According to the Statement, if there is uncertainty about an item's continued existence, derecognition will not take place until sufficient evidence exists that a transaction or other event has eliminated the item (SP, 5.24). This introduces a degree of asymmetry into the system since if the item had not previously been recognized it would not, under these circumstances, now be recognized; yet, because it has been recognized, it remains in the financial statements. Where the item no longer satisfies the recognition criteria, it should be derecognized even if there has been no change in its inherent nature. This means that if events now mean that there is insufficient evidence that the asset or liability was created, or if it cannot now be measured with sufficient reliability, it will be derecognized. The Statement of Principles emphasizes that these occasions will be rare.

Recognition and contemporary practice

Matching

We have seen (Chapter 6) that the 'strong-form' interpretation of matching implicit in some contemporary accounting practices is inconsistent with the approach of the Statement of Principles. The Statement does, however, use matching in various ways that are subsidiary to element definition and the recognition criteria. Derecognition at a single point in time where the asset or liability is eliminated at a single point in time is consistent with matching. Where an asset is eliminated over several periods (for example, where a fixed tangible item such as plant and machinery is used up over several periods), derecognition over those periods is achieved by matching, normally by recognizing the loss (depreciation) on a systematic basis over the periods in which the benefits are delivered up.

The operating cycle

Contemporary accounting practice often involves recognizing revenue on the basis of the business's operating cycle. Specifically, profit is recognized when the critical event in the cycle has been achieved. For example, it is considered that the critical event in a normal manufacturing and sales cycle is making the sale: merely manufacturing a particular batch of goods does not give sufficient assurance that it will be possible to sell them at a profit, whereas actually selling them at a profitable price does normally provide assurance that the profit will be achieved because, in a sophisticated market economy, debtors do normally settle their debts and so the proceeds of the sale will be received.

The Statement of Principles views the *critical event* as 'the point in an operating cycle at which there will usually be sufficient evidence that the gain exists and it will usually be possible to measure that gain with sufficient reliability' (SP, 5.34). On this view, the critical event is the point at which the Statement's own recognition criteria are met and hence the critical event approach is consistent with the Statement. Alternative interpretations of the critical event approach, such as the view that the critical event is 'the point in the operating cycle when the most critical decision is made or the most critical act is performed' (Davies et al., 1999: 171), might not be so completely consistent with the Statement's recognition criteria. It also needs to be borne in mind that it would not be consistent with the Statement *always* to recognize profit at the critical event, as defined in the Statement. This is because that definition refers to the point at which there is *usually* sufficient evidence and the possibility of measurement with sufficient reliability. Thus if, for a particular item, the critical event passed but there was insufficient evidence of the existence of an asset or liability, or it was not possible to measure the item with sufficient reliability, the Statement of Principles would require that the item was not recognized; whereas, if the policy was to recognize profit on the critical event, it presumably would be recognized.

Prudence

We saw in Chapter 3 that the notion of prudence adopted by the Statement of Principles is that a degree of caution should be exercised in the face of uncertainty to ensure that gains and assets are not overstated and losses and liabilities are not understated, but that this should not extend to deliberately understating gains and assets or deliberately overstating losses and liabilities. In recognizing gains and losses, the Statement explains that prudence should be achieved by:

1 requiring more confirmatory evidence about the existence of a gain or asset than about the existence of a loss or liability; and
2 requiring greater reliability of measurement for gains and assets than for losses and liabilities.

While this approach looks quite close to contemporary practice, there is a fine line between not deliberately understating assets and requiring more confirmatory evidence and greater reliability of measurement for assets than for liabilities. Some commentators have argued that the Statement's approach to prudence in recognition undermines its position on neutrality as a desirable qualitative characteristic of financial information.

Going concern

One of the four fundamental accounting concepts incorporated into SSAP2 and company law is *going concern*. Under the going concern concept, financial statements are prepared on the assumption that 'the enterprise will continue in operational existence for the foreseeable future' (SSAP2, paragraph 14(a)). Whether or not an entity is a going concern will also have a significant influence on the recognition process as set out in the Statement of Principles. For example, an entity which ceases to be a going concern may find that there is no longer sufficient evidence that it can obtain economic benefits embodied in previously recognized assets, for example it may no longer be able to expect to sell specialist stock.

Applications

Development expenditure

SSAP13 permits (but does not require) entities to capitalize development expenditure under certain circumstances. We have already seen that the tests to be applied under SSAP13 can be seen as primarily concerned to address the issue of whether a given project in its development stage meets the definition of an asset (see Chapter 4), but they also have a bearing on the recognition criteria. In particular, examining expenditure project by project (clause (a) of the tests) will help in establishing that there is sufficient evidence that an asset has been created and that it can be measured reliably. Separate identification of expenditure (clause (b)) will also aid reliable measurement. Thus, the tests set out in SSAP13 can be viewed as operationalizing the recognition criteria in the Statement of Principles, although they were in fact set down well before work on the Statement of Principles began.

Long-term contracts

In most industries, an entity's sales consist of individual units or batches, manufactured and sold within a short period of time and with large numbers of sales made in any period, to many different customers. In some industries, however, an entity's sales will consist of a small number of contracts, each of which may be carried out over a period of years. An example is the civil engineering sector: one contractor may be working on only a handful of projects, perhaps a couple of motorways and a hospital, with each project expected to last several years.

Traditionally, accountants recognized the profit on these projects on the *completed contracts* basis, that is the whole profit on the contract was recognized in the period in which the project was completed. It was argued that this could be justified on the grounds of prudence, as then interpreted, because until the project was virtually complete, the contractor could not be sure that unforeseen snags had been avoided, and the emergence of such snags would increase costs and reduce or eliminate the profit margin. Put another way, completion was argued to be the critical event. It could also be justified by appealing to a parallel with profit recognition on ordinary manufacturing, since handing over the completed project to the customer can be seen as equivalent to physically delivering goods.

However there were a number of problems associated with the completed contracts method. A company could be working for a full accounting period on several extremely lucrative contracts, yet if none of them were completed during the period it would show no profit for that period. In another period it might complete several contracts and record a profit much more substantial than it could possibly repeat in future years. Finally, since the point at which a large project is regarded as completed is to some degree arbitrary, and can also be controlled by management (by accelerating or delaying the final stage of the work), management have a considerable degree of discretion about the profit they declare in any period.

As a result of concerns about the completed contracts basis, SSAP9, originally issued in 1975, required the use of the *percentage of completion* method, under which profit is recognized as the work progresses. The advantage of this method is that the profit and loss account for the period reflects the work undertaken by the entity for the period, rather than the, relatively arbitrary, incidence of contract completion dates. It can thus form a much better guide to future earning capacity. Arguably, therefore, the method aids estimation of future earnings and cash flow and thus provides relevant information. The question is whether the gains arising under this method satisfy the recognition criteria in the Statement of Principles.

The Statement of Principles argues that they do, citing the critical event approach discussed earlier:

> The operating cycle might involve a contract that is performed in stages, for each of which there is a critical event. (Contracts to build large buildings are usually an example of such an operating cycle.) In such circumstances, the gain that is expected to be earned on the contract as a whole will need to be allocated among the critical events. (SP, 5.36(c))

On the other hand, some critics of the Statement of Principles take the opposite view:

> We find it somewhat surprising that the ASB believes that the application of the percentage-of-completion method of profit recognition in the case of long-

term construction contracts is an example of the critical event approach . . . this is clearly an application of the accretion approach, and the ASB's confusion on the matter seems to illustrate . . . its inability to devise a theoretically coherent conceptual framework. (Davies et al., 1999: 177)

Davies et al. regard the accretion approach, under which gains are recognized 'during the process of "production", rather than at the end of a contract or when production is complete' (1999: 178), as an alternative to the critical event approach and suggest that, under current GAAP, this approach is employed for long-term contracts, the use by others of an entity's resources (so that it applies for rental payments, interest income, and so on) and natural growth biological transformation (accounting for livestock, forests, and the like).

It does seem that to make the percentage of completion method an application of the critical event approach it is necessary to accept that there can be not one but many critical events in a single transaction. This view makes it difficult to distinguish the critical event approach from any other method of recognizing gains, since, in effect, the transaction or other event that is going to trigger off recognition is deemed to be a critical event and thus the critical event approach becomes simply another way of describing the recognition criteria, rather than an independent method that meets the criteria. Equally, appeals to faithful representation and substance do not always resolve practical problems where gains and losses, which do not necessarily have physical manifestations, are involved: different individuals may have different views on whether the gain on a long-term contract arises slowly over time or at a particular point. What this demonstrates is not that the Statement of Principles is wrong but that applying a conceptual framework is the beginning rather than the end of the process of developing accounting standards rigorously.

Hedges of contracted future transactions

We examined in Chapter 6 the nature of hedging and the problems that arise in the context of uncontracted future transactions. We can now look at the position where the hedged item is a contracted future transaction. Let us take, for example, the case of an operating lease held by an entity where the future rental payments will be made in a foreign currency. In order to reduce or eliminate its exposure to the risk of future movements in the exchange rate the entity acquires, now, contracts entitling it to purchase the necessary foreign exchange, at the times at which it will be needed, at rates fixed in the contracts.

Under current GAAP the future obligations under the operating lease are not recognized in the balance sheet (see Chapter 4). If the financial instruments constituting the hedge were accounted for separately, gains and losses coming about as the exchange rate moved (and the entity's rights to obtain future currency became worth more or less in terms of sterling) could be recognized as the exchange rate movements occurred and not in the same period as the lease payments had to be made. Thus, for example, if the movement was such that the foreign currency cost more in pounds, the entity would recognize a gain when the movement occurred (because its right to obtain currency at the previous rate would be worth more) but would then show a higher cost for the lease payment in the period in which that payment was made. Under current GAAP, the entity could use hedge accounting, deferring recognition of the gain on the contract to purchase foreign currency (the financial instrument) until the lease payment is recognized.

In this case, hedge accounting is being used to compensate for differences in the timing of recognition of the lease payment and the gain on the hedge under GAAP. One approach would be to recognize the current obligation to make future lease payments as a liability so that both the obligation and the asset that hedges it (the financial instrument) are recognized, and this is what the approach of the Statement of Principles would lead to (see Chapter 4). If this is not done, how should the hedge be accounted for?

The problems of hedge accounting for contracted future transactions are a good example of the difficulties of arriving at consistency once anomalous treatments have crept into the system. In this case the anomaly is that contracted future obligations (operating lease payments) are not recognized under GAAP. If we treat gains and losses on financial instruments that are hedges consistently with the hedged item (deferring gains and losses), we are treating them inconsistently with economically identical financial instruments that are not hedges (the gains and losses on which will be recognized as the exchange rate movements occur). However, if we recognize the gains and losses on all financial instruments consistently, we recognize in different periods the items that management actually intended to align against each other when they designed the hedge.

One set of arguments in favour of hedge accounting is drawn from strong-form matching: it is claimed that the gain or loss on the hedge should be matched to the hedged item. A defence of this view is that the intention of the hedge (and its result if it is successful) is to reduce the variability of overall cash flows and it should thus not introduce volatility into the profit and loss account. This approach could be argued to be more relevant in indicating the pattern of cash flows that might be expected in future.

The Statement of Principles, as we have seen (see Chapter 3), adopts the qualitative characteristic of reliability and hence faithful representation, and if this is applied to individual categories of assets and liabilities, it will lead to accounting for the hedge in the same way as other economically similar financial instruments. On the other hand, if the quality of faithful representation is applied to the totality of the hedging arrangement, it could become an argument for hedge accounting.

Another set of arguments relates to the behavioural consequences of permitting, or not permitting, hedge accounting. It is sometimes suggested that not permitting hedge accounting would discourage management from undertaking hedging at all, since the consequent limitation in the variability of cash flows would not be apparent in the financial statements. In addition, users might be misled and take inappropriate economic decisions – for example believing that the gain resulting from the rise in the value of the hedge in the example discussed above would be sustained period by period as an increase in overall profitability when in fact, if all else remains the same, profitability will fall as a result of the increased cost of the lease payments in future years. These arguments in effect suggest that the accounting treatments to be used should be worked back from the desired effect on behaviour – a form of social engineering. We have already examined this argument (see Chapter 2). Counter-arguments in the case of hedge accounting include the view that it is for users to decide whether hedging is desirable and that they should be shown the consequences of the hedging (the gain or loss on the hedge at the time the exchange rate moves) and left to decide whether they agree with management's actions. It is not necessarily self-evident that hedging is valuable to users: for example, they may be able to diversify the risk attaching to future cash flows better themselves, and using financial instruments to hedge may introduce other forms of risk, such as the danger that the counterparty to the instrument may default.

Contingencies

The difficulties which financial reporting has in dealing with contingencies illustrate well the problems resulting from uncertainty. According to the *New Oxford Dictionary of English*, a contingency is 'a future event or circumstance which is possible but cannot be predicted with certainty'. A common example of a contingency in accounting is the situation in which a company is being sued, say in a product liability case, and does not know the outcome at the balance sheet date. If the court finds in its favour, the cost may be small; if the court finds against it, it may have to pay damages running into millions of pounds. Until very recently the accounting standard applicable to contingencies was SSAP18, which defined a contingency as:

> a condition which exists at the balance sheet date, where the outcome will be confirmed only on the occurrence or non-occurrence of one or more uncertain future events. (paragraph 14)

This definition is equivalent to the normal dictionary definition. SSAP18 went on to define 'a contingent gain or loss' as 'a gain or loss dependent on a contingency' (paragraph 14). Under the standard, contingent losses had to be recognized where it was

> probable that a future event [would] confirm a loss which can be estimated with reasonable accuracy at the date on which the financial statements are approved. (paragraph 15)

Contingent gains were not permitted to be recognized, an approach consistent with the traditional operation of the concept of prudence.

Most accountants had little difficulty understanding what SSAP18 was driving at. However, its terminology, at least, is inconsistent with an economic view of financial statement elements, and thus with the Statement of Principles, given that 'entities operate in an uncertain environment' (SP, 5.8).

Contingent gains and losses are associated with contingent assets and liabilities (the contingent loss arising from the damages in the example given above is also a contingent liability for the company) and, since the Statement of Principles focuses on assets and liabilities, we will discuss contingencies in terms of assets and liabilities rather than gains and losses. The consequences of this switch, which is mirrored in the new accounting standard dealing with contingencies (FRS12), are not significant.

Let us focus on contingent liabilities. Remember that liabilities involve obligations to transfer economic benefits as a result of past events. The transfer of benefits will occur at some point in the future. In an uncertain environment there will be some uncertainty, however tiny, attaching to any future event. Hence, strictly speaking, all liabilities are contingent liabilities on the definition in SSAP18. Even a straightforward trade creditor is contingent in the sense that the outcome of the liability (its settlement) will be confirmed only on the non-occurrence of a variety of possible future events, such as the waiving of the debt by the creditor or the entity losing contact with the creditor in such a way that it is not practicable to settle the debt. These events occur so infrequently in practice that a trade creditor is, for all practical purposes, a liability known with certainty, but conceptually, like all other assets and liabilities, it is uncertain and thus contingent.

The new accounting standard dealing with contingencies, FRS12, defines a contingent liability as:

(a) a possible obligation that arises from past events and whose existence will be confirmed only by the occurrence of one or more uncertain future events not wholly within the entity's control; or

(b) a present obligation that arises from past events but is not recognised because:

   (i) it is not probable that a transfer of economic benefits will be required to settle the obligation; or

   (ii) the amount of the obligation cannot be measured with sufficient reliability. (paragraph 2)

Under FRS12, contingent liabilities are *not* recognized in the financial statements (though they may well have to be disclosed).

The FRS12 definition seeks to set out the position in the context of a more realistic approach to uncertainty. Clause (a) focuses on uncertainty about the *existence* of the obligation rather than merely its outcome. The FRS takes the view (see FRS12, Appendix III, Example 10) that where, in a current court case, it is probable that an entity will not be found liable, no obligation exists as a result of past events. The obligation that would result from an adverse finding is thus a possible obligation meeting the terms of clause (a) and hence is a contingent liability but would not be recognized because, under FRS12, contingent liabilities are not recognized. This contrasts with the previous position under SSAP18: the adverse finding would have satisfied the definition of a contingent loss (the condition, the court case, existed at the balance sheet date and the outcome would be confirmed by the uncertain future event of the court's findings) but would not have been recognized because it was not probable that a future event (the findings) would confirm a loss. Thus the actual accounting numbers would be the same in both cases.

Equally, had it been probable that the court would find against the entity, the accounting numbers in the financial statements would have been the same but the route to them would have been different. Under SSAP18 there would have been a contingent loss, recognized because it was probable that the future event would confirm it. Under FRS12 there is a present obligation on the basis of the evidence available, and hence it is recognized in the normal way: there is no contingent liability but rather a liability.

Clause (b)(ii) addresses, fairly straightforwardly, the, no doubt very rare, case where an obligation fails the recognition criterion relating to measurement. Clause (b)(i) is something of a half-way house. The kind of obligation that might be covered by this clause would be a debt to a public sector body that was legally enforceable at the date of the financial statements but for which there was substantial evidence that it would in fact be waived, perhaps on the basis of precedents in other cases, government statements, and so on. Strictly speaking, the obligations here could satisfy both the definition of a liability and the recognition criteria (there may be plenty of evidence that they exist and they may be easy to measure). Nonetheless, it is easy to see why it would not be useful to recognize them. Under the US conceptual framework, which defines liabilities in terms of 'probable future sacrifices of economic benefits arising from present obligations' (SFAC6, paragraph 35), the problem would not have arisen because the item would not have satisfied the definition of a liability. Under the UK approach, it is necessary to take something that, strictly speaking, satisfies the definition of a liability and the recognition criteria, then define it as a contingent liability and establish a standard that contingent liabilities are not recognized.

The wording of FRS12 is clearly different to that of its predecessor standard, and is more complex and does not relate easily to a lay person's normal understanding of contingency. However, as we have seen, SSAP18's approach and the normal dictionary definition of contingency themselves cause conceptual difficulties when it is accepted that all assets and liabilities have a measure of uncertainty attaching to them.

Intangibles purchased as part of a business

FRS10 requires that intangibles acquired as part of the acquisition of a business should be capitalized separately from goodwill if their value can be measured reliably on initial recognition (paragraph 10: see Chapter 4). This is an application of the recognition criteria, albeit a somewhat unusual one, in that, if the intangible fails the test for recognition as a separate asset, it will be subsumed within goodwill and included in the balance sheet anyway. Hence the issue here is the kind of asset being recognized rather than the resulting balance sheet total.

Internally generated intangibles

Under FRS10, internally generated intangibles can be recognized as assets only where they have a readily ascertainable market value (paragraph 14). This may appear at first sight to be an application of the measurability criterion for recognition but it is a restrictive application of that criterion and FRS10 recognizes this (Appendix III, paragraph 25), arguing that the treatment of the general run of internally generated intangibles should be aligned to the treatment of internally generated goodwill, because of the similarity in their nature, and also because measuring the value of most intangibles is subjective.

The ASB is keen to align the treatment of internally generated intangibles with that of internally generated goodwill because of the difficulty of distinguishing in practice between them, and the consequent danger that, if different treatments were permitted, companies would classify items as goodwill or intangibles in order to achieve the treatment they wished. As we have seen, the ASB considers that goodwill is not an asset, although the US standard-setting body argues that it is (Chapter 4). Again, we can see that adopting a conceptual framework may help in developing standards but it by no means makes the rest of the task a foregone conclusion.

Notes

1 The Statement of Principles also discusses executory (unperformed) contracts at this point but we have already examined this issue (see Chapter 4).

References

Davies, M., Paterson, R. and Wilson, A. (1999) *UK GAAP*, 6th edn. London: Macmillan.

Further reading

For a discussion of recognition, see D. Solomons, *Making Accounting Policy: the Quest for Credibility in Financial Reporting*, Oxford: OUP, 1986, Chapter 6.

For an analysis of GAAP on contingencies, see M. Davies, R. Paterson and A. Wilson, *UK GAAP*, 6th edn, London: Macmillan, 1999.

8

Measurement

We have seen that *measurement* is the last stage in arriving at the accounting numbers that appear in financial statements: an item must first meet the definition of a statement element; the recognition criteria must then be satisfied; finally it is measured. In examining measurement, the Statement of Principles focuses on the debate between two *measurement bases*, namely *historical cost* and *current value*, while conceding that each of these itself has variants (SP, 6.1). The Statement requires that the measurement basis employed for each category of assets and liabilities should be selected to meet the objective of financial statements and the demands of the qualitative characteristics of financial information. It points out that there are two possible approaches to the specification of a measurement basis. A single basis could be specified to apply for all categories of asset and liability or a measurement basis could be specified separately for each category of assets and liabilities, yielding a *mixed measurement system*. It envisages that the latter approach will be adopted, combining historical cost and current value.

In this chapter we will examine the Statement of Principles' discussion of the measurement process and the criteria it specifies for choosing and changing measurement bases. The Statement also contains some discussion of the methods to be used under the current value measurement basis which are outside the scope of this text.

The measurement process

Initial recognition

Under historical cost, an asset or a liability acquired by a transaction is recognized at the transaction cost, which is the fair value of the consideration given or received in exchange for the asset or liability. Assets and liabilities acquired as a result of other events are recognized at fair value. Under current value an asset or a liability is recognized at current value. Hence, where transactions are carried out at fair value their initial recognition will be at the same amount under both historical cost and current value because the transaction cost will equal the fair value of the consideration, which will itself equal the current value of the asset or liability. This will apply to the large majority of transactions undertaken by profit-seeking entities with third parties.

Unless there is evidence to the contrary, it can generally be assumed that a transaction has been carried out at fair value. Initial recognition can therefore take place on the basis of the fair value of either the asset or liability acquired or the consideration given or received, whichever is the easier to measure. If a transaction was not carried out at fair value (for example, a donation to a not-for-profit entity), the Statement indicates that current value will often be the more appropriate measurement basis.

We have already examined the recognition criteria to be applied at initial recognition (see Chapter 7). Whether a measure has sufficient reliability for inclusion in the financial statements will depend on the quantity and quality of evidence concerning its reliability, as defined in the Statement of Principles. As the Statement puts it:

> A measure derived from a generally accepted valuation methodology and supported by a reasonable amount of confirmatory evidence will usually be a sufficiently reliable measure. (SP, 6.16)

Subsequent remeasurement

The Statement points out that in a strictly pure historical cost system, there is no subsequent remeasurement: all amounts are left at the amount at which they are initially recognized until they are derecognized. Adjustments to carrying amounts to reflect additional costs (for example during conversion of raw materials into finished goods by the application of labour) and allocation (for example, depreciation) are not remeasurements but rather are necessary to maintain assets and liabilities at historical cost. However, as the Statement also points out, such a pure system is not in fact used and the Statement's discussion of historical cost deals with the system as normally employed. This system uses remeasurement to reduce assets to recoverable amount where this is below historical cost (for example, stating stock at the lower of cost and market value) and to translate monetary assets and liabilities denominated in foreign currencies at up-to-date exchange rates.

Where the current value measurement basis is employed, remeasurement is carried out systematically to keep current values up to date.

Remeasurement is subject to recognition criteria which are broadly similar to those applying at the initial recognition stage. Remeasurements are recognized only if: (a) there is sufficient evidence that the amount of the asset or liability has changed; and (b) the new amount is capable of being measured with sufficient reliability. Thus, for example, in examining a possible write-down of stock to recoverable amount under the historical cost basis, criterion (a) will mean that it will be necessary to examine evidence that recoverable amount is below historical cost.

What constitutes sufficient evidence will be a matter of judgement in individual cases: it will often not be possible to identify conclusive evidence and this is not necessary. According to the Statement,

> relevant considerations as to whether the evidence is sufficient will include its persuasiveness and whether the change implies that a gain or loss has occurred. (SP, 6.20)

It is not clear whether the latter clause is to be taken to mean that losses should be recognized on less evidence than gains (as an application of prudence) or that any change involving gains or losses (as opposed to one accompanied by an opposite change in another asset or liability so that the effect on ownership interest was balanced) requires a different weight of evidence for recognition.

The primary source of evidence will be past or current experience with the item itself or similar items. Evidence may include: (a) current information relating to the item (for example, the physical condition of stock); (b) other entities' transactions in similar items; and (c) past experience with similar items (for example the age of a similar item of plant). The weight of evidence which emerges from other entities' transactions will depend on whether there is an active market in similar items (in which case the quality of the evidence is likely to be good) or whether the market is thin or items are not fully comparable (in which case the evidence will be less persuasive). Issues relating to the reliability of remeasurement are the same as those arising on initial recognition and discussed earlier in this chapter.

Choosing and changing a measurement basis

The Statement of Principles requires that:

> In choosing the measurement basis to be used for a particular category of assets or liabilities, the aim is to select the basis that is most appropriate bearing in mind:
>
> (a) the objective of financial statements and the qualitative characteristics of financial information, in particular relevance and reliability;
> (b) the nature of the assets or liabilities concerned; and
> (c) the particular circumstances involved. (SP, 6.23)

It goes on to say that 'it is often difficult to make general statements about the appropriate measurement basis for any particular category of assets or liabilities' but offers some 'observations' (SP, 6.25).

These observations follow from the Statement's approach to relevance and reliability (see Chapter 3). The focus in making a choice will be on usefulness. If only one measurement basis is reliable, it will be used as long as it is also relevant. If both historical cost and current value are reliable, the more relevant should be chosen. The Statement argues that, although it is sometimes said that current values are less reliable than historical cost, such an assertion can be based on the misconception that historical cost measures are always derived from transactions when in fact they are often remeasurements not based on actual transactions, such as carrying amounts written down to recoverable value (a point we have encountered before: see Chapter 4). Assessments of relevance and reliability need to take account of the nature of the relevant assets or liabilities: for example, if an entity holds surplus liquidity in the form of an investment, the relevance of the investment to the entity is derived from its ability to generate cash flows, and the most faithful representation of the right to those flows is likely to be current value. Finally, the answers that emerge from applying the tests of the best measurement basis specified in the Statement and set out above may change over time; for example as markets develop, so that similar items are traded more frequently and the differences in price which result from minor differences between items are easier to observe, a measurement basis that was once unreliable for lack of evidence may become sufficiently reliable for use.

Measurement uncertainty

The measurement of a financial statement element will usually involve some degree of uncertainty about what the appropriate monetary amount is. This is addressed in the recognition criteria for initial recognition and for remeasurement, which require that an element can be recognized or remeasured only if the amount can be measured with sufficient reliability.

Measurement in the face of uncertainty requires the use of estimation and, where a generally acceptable method of estimation is used and reasonable supporting evidence is available, the use of estimation does not prevent the measure from being sufficiently reliable to be used in financial statements. Estimation can involve the use of market values where a reasonably efficient market exists so that a consensus view of the benefits embodied in the item can be observed. Where a large number of homogeneous items are held, it may be possible to arrive at a reliable estimate of the measure of the whole group even when the outcomes associated with each individual member are highly uncertain. For example, it may be easier to estimate what proportion of trade debts will not be received than to say which particular debtors will not pay. If neither of these approaches is practicable the Statement of Principles argues that a best estimate will need to be used. If there is a minimum amount that is reasonably assured, the item will be stated at no less than that minimum amount, and a higher amount will be used if that is a better estimate. (SP, 6.37(c))

No further guidance on what constitutes the 'best estimate' is given.

The mixed measurement basis and current practice

As the Statement points out (SP, Appendix III, paragraph 51), the majority of large companies now use in their published financial statements a combination of historical costs and current values. The system is usually referred to in practice as *modified historical cost* but this can be argued to be a somewhat misleading term, since the modification involves using a different measurement basis, and the Statement prefers to use the term 'mixed measurement basis'. Thus the system that the Statement 'envisages' (SP, 6.4) will be used is consistent with current GAAP, as employed by large companies, though whether, within this system, the best choices between historical cost and current value are being made is open to question. The application of the tests to be used in determining the best measurement basis under the mixed measurement system could, in principle, yield the same basis for all assets and liabilities, so it could be argued that an entity using historical cost was complying with the tests if it could show that in all cases the best method was, indeed, historical cost.

The Statement explicitly rules out the use of a system under which categories of assets and liabilities would be measured at some point at current value and then left at that amount for long periods or indefinitely, with the consequence that they are stated neither at historical cost nor at current value as at the date of the financial statements. It does so on the grounds that this will 'disturb the comparability and consistency of accounting measurement' (SP, 6.5) and hence not conform to the principles set out in the Statement. This rules out the practice of occasional revaluation, permitted under GAAP until the adoption of FRS15 in 2000.

The Statement explicitly states that:

it is unlikely that the framework [of tests for selecting the best measurement basis] . . . will suggest the use of current values other than for certain types of investments, commodity stocks and financial instruments. (SP, Appendix III, paragraph 59)

Criticisms of the approach to measurement

Criticisms of the Statement of Principles' consideration of measurement fall into two categories. At a technical level, the amount and rigour of the analysis is fairly limited. Although the Statement sets out the aim in selecting a measurement basis, as we have seen, it concludes that it is 'difficult to make general statements' about which basis will be appropriate for particular categories of assets and liabilities and merely offers some 'observations' (SP, 6.25). Yet measurement is the vital last stage in actually arriving at the accounting numbers in financial statements, so that a conceptual framework which does not make general statements about the choice of a measurement basis for individual categories of assets and liabilities is stopping somewhat short of the desired destination.

Commenting on the US framework's coverage of recognition and measurement, David Solomons concluded that:

> Under a rigorous grading system I would give [the chapters] an F and require the board to take the course over again – that is, to scrap the [contents] and start afresh. (1986: 124)

Some commentators have offered a similar conclusion about the UK Statement of Principles (see, for example, Baxter, 1999).

One possible reason for the limited content of the measurement chapter is the need to strike a political balance between those who favour historical cost and those who advocate current value. Perhaps predictably, the outcome has come under attack from both directions. The 1995 exposure draft of the Statement of Principles appeared to advance the case for current value accounting rather more strongly than the final version and was attacked by some commentators for its 'unwarranted faith in current values' (Ernst and Young, 1996: 9). The more neutral position of the later exposure draft was welcomed by those commentators, though doubts were expressed about whether the change 'represents a true ASB conviction, or . . . has just been included as a tactical ploy in order to forestall any potential criticism' (Davies et al., 1999: 135). The Statement of Principles itself says very firmly that to

> have assumed the adoption of a comprehensive current value system . . . would have been a revolutionary step and [such a system] is not an approach that the Board has considered in the past nor is it one that it expects to consider in the foreseeable future. (SP, Appendix III, paragraph 54(b))

The weakening in the argument for current value has, needless to say, attracted criticism from those who advocate this system:

> While I understand the board's wish to avoid stirring up an emotion-charged controversy over historical cost v. current value, so that it can move towards the final approval of its conceptual framework, it has preferred to relegate this important choice from one of principle to one of interpretation. It is most unfortunate that the board has not provided more forceful, principled guidance . . . Some of the most vexing issues in financial accounting in the US

are traceable to the deficiencies of historical cost . . . the ASB's climb-down on current value accounting is happening at a time when an eloquent and coherent statement of principle is needed. (Zeff, 1999: 81)

On balance, it may be that the Statement's relatively neutral stance on measurement is necessary to achieve the adoption of a conceptual framework that offers substantial benefits in the other areas that need to be addressed in setting standards, such as element definition and recognition. However, there is little doubt that it will simply leave battles to be fought during the development of the standards themselves.

References

Baxter, W. (1999) 'The ASB on principles', *Accountancy*, October: 75–6.
Davies, M., Paterson, R. and Wilson, A. (1999) *UK GAAP*, 6th edn. London: Macmillan.
Ernst and Young (1996) *The ASB's Framework: Time to Debate*. London: Ernst and Young.
Solomons, D. (1986) 'The FASB's conceptual framework: an evaluation', *Journal of Accountancy*, June: 114–24.
Zeff, S. (1999) 'Sitting on the fence', *Accountancy*, July: 81.

Further reading

For critical analyses of the ASB's approach to measurement, see W. Baxter, 'The ASB on principles', *Accountancy*, October 1999, pp. 75–6; and S. Zeff, 'Sitting on the fence', *Accountancy*, July 1999, p. 81.

9

Presentation of Financial Information

We have now seen how, according to the Statement of Principles, the accounting numbers in a set of financial statements should be derived. The final stage in preparing financial information is to decide how it should be presented.

A classification of financial information

We can classify the financial information that is useful for taking economic decisions as follows:

1   Annual general purpose financial reports (and other similar reports) prepared by entities, which comprise:
   (a)   The general purpose financial statements, which comprise:
      (i)   The general purpose primary financial statements:
- The statement of financial performance, which may in practice be broken down into two or more separate statements. The most important statement of financial performance in current GAAP is generally known as the profit and loss account. Whether an entity produces a single overall statement of financial performance, or several dealing with different aspects of performance, is a question of detail and legal requirement that does not raise any issues of principle.
- The statement of financial position (usually referred to as the balance sheet).
- The cash flow statement.

      (ii)   The notes to the financial statements, which amplify the information contained in the primary financial statements and supplement them.
   (b)   Information accompanying the financial statements, such as the operating and financial review and the directors' report.

2   Other general purpose financial reports, such as letters to share-holders and press releases.
3   Other means of providing information useful for economic decision-making outside the general purpose financial reporting process, such as special purpose financial statements, financial analysts' reports, economic statistics about the industrial sector in which the entity is located, general news stories about the entity, and so on.

Although the Statement of Principles concentrates largely on the general purpose primary financial reports, the specification of these statements needs to take into account their use as part of a wider package of information. The Statement includes some guidance on the content of accompanying information but this is outside the scope of this text.

Presentation of information in financial statements

According to the Statement, the objective to be pursued in presenting information in financial statements is

> to communicate clearly and effectively and in as simple and straightforward a manner as is possible without loss of relevance or reliability and without unnecessarily increasing the length of the financial statements. (SP, 7.1)

It is a characteristic of financial statements that information is presented in a highly structured and aggregated way: even if it was possible to report separately each transaction and other event taking place in a period this would not satisfy the objective of financial reporting. The processes of 'interpretation, simplification, abstraction and aggregation' (SP, 7.2) that are involved in preparing highly structured financial statements involve a loss of detailed information but facilitate effective communication to users by: (a) bringing to the fore information that would otherwise be obscured; (b) highlighting significant items and relationships; (c) enhancing comparability; and (d) improving under-standability.

The notes to the primary financial statement form part of an integrated whole with the statements themselves. The notes may include detailed breakdowns of totals presented in the statements, to avoid cluttering up the face of the statements and thus promote clear communication. They may also be used to present alternative interpretations, such as seg-mental analysis of the aggregates in the statements or a comment on possible outcomes of a legal dispute other than that assumed in the statements themselves. Finally they may include information that cannot be included in the financial statements because the recognition criteria have not been met, perhaps because of uncertainty.

A key aspect of the process of preparing highly structured information is the use of *classification*. In the words of the Statement of Principles, 'items that are similar are presented together in the financial statement and distinguished from dissimilar items' (SP, 7.6). The classifications adopted should also have regard to the usefulness of comparing different classes of item. The Statement of Principles gives as an example here, debtors and sales. The argument would be that in classifying current assets, it is useful to distinguish debtors so that a user can calculate, for example, the collection period. However, it is interesting to note that in contemporary GAAP, the sales figure is not broken down between credit and cash sales so that the collection period calculation is potentially flawed where an entity makes a significant volume of cash sales. The classification system used in financial statements is hierarchical: that is, not only are items grouped into classes but classes are then grouped together, again on the basis of similarity of nature or relationship. Thus, for example, the various classes of current assets are themselves grouped together and a subtotal is struck to provide an aggregate figure for current assets.

Good presentation

Statement of financial performance

An entity's overall financial performance in a period can be analysed into components with differing characteristics in terms of, for example:

1   The nature of the items, for example, employment costs, interest payable, and so on.
2   Cause, for example whether costs vary with volume.
3   Function, for example, production, administration, and so on.
4   Likelihood that items will recur in future periods, for example trading activities are likely to continue in future periods whereas the failure of a major trade debtor requiring a very substantial write-off is more likely to be a 'one-off' occurrence.
5   Stability, for example sales to a domestic market may be less likely to fluctuate than exports.
6   Riskiness.
7   Predictability.
8   Reliability.

All components of financial performance will be relevant to users of the financial statements, and should thus be reported, but some will carry more weight in the assessment of performance than others. For example, users wanting to forecast the following period's performance will clearly attach more weight to components that are likely to recur, and will have more confidence in a forecast of components that have been shown to be relatively stable.

The presentation of information on financial performance should focus attention on the components of performance and on the key characteristics of those components. The Statement of Principles indicates that good presentation 'typically involves' (SP, 7.10):

1   Recognizing only gains and losses in the statement of financial performance.
2   Classifying components by a combination of function and nature.
3   Distinguishing amounts that are affected in different ways by changes in economic conditions or business activity, for example giving segmental breakdowns and separating out the performance of operations that have been discontinued during the period.
4   Separately identifying items that are unusual in amount or incidence, items that have special characteristics (such as financing costs and taxation), and items related primarily to future profits (such as some research and development expenditure).

We have seen that, under the Statement of Principles, a gain is defined in terms of an increase in ownership interest other than a contribution from owners and that the Statement interprets this to mean that, for example, on a sale of stock, the gross revenue is treated as a gain and the accompanying reduction in stock (and thus ownership interest) is treated as a loss (see Chapter 6). What we would normally think of as the profit on this sale is, in the terms of the Statement, the net result of the gross gain and loss. The Statement considers that whether the gross gain and loss should be offset in the financial statements is a presentation issue (SP, 4.41). The Statement indicates that gains and losses are generally *not* offset but will be if they relate to the same event or circumstance, and disclosing the gross amounts is not likely to be useful for assessing future results or the effect of past transactions or events. The normal presentation of sales in the profit and loss account, that is showing sales less cost of sales to yield profit, is presumably a case where disclosing the components separately is likely to be useful. By contrast, the profit made on disposal of a fixed asset is shown as a net amount because this is more useful.

Balance sheet

According to the Statement of Principles:

> In assessing the financial position of an entity, users are most interested in the types and amounts of assets and liabilities held and the relationship between them, and in the function of the various assets. (SP, 7.12)

Accordingly, good presentation 'typically involves' (SP, 7.12):

1   Recognizing only assets, liabilities and ownership interest in the balance sheet.
2   Classifying assets and liabilities so as to delineate the resource structure (assets) and financial structure (liabilities and ownership interest) of the entity. This involves enabling the user to assess the nature, amount and liquidity of resources, the nature, amount and timing of obligations, and the function of assets.

Assets and liabilities are not offset (see Chapter 5).

Cash flow statement

The Statement of Principles argues that cash flow information will be most useful if it distinguishes between (a) generation and use of cash; and (b) flows from operations amd other flows.

Applications

Segmental information

Segmental reports disaggregate overall information covering the entity in its entirety between different areas of operation, classically classes of business or geographical regions. The information covered in a segmental report mirrors that provided in the primary financial statements and can thus involve financial performance, position and cash flow. The importance of segmental information for an entity operating across two or more areas is that it enhances users' ability to make the assessments they need for decision-making. For example, in forecasting the following year's earnings, it may be useful to see what proportion of the current period's earnings comes from sectors which are themselves likely to grow and what proportion from sectors which may be stable or in decline. Many forecasting models use information disaggregated below the level of the data to be predicted, building the prediction up from components rather than simply extrapolating values of the variable which is the subject of the prediction.

Hence, segmental information is a way of presenting accompanying information, alongside the primary financial statements, which clearly enhances the value of the information in accordance with the Statement of Principles' guidelines. UK GAAP (company law and SSAP25) includes a requirement to provide segmental information embracing sales, results and net assets on both a class of business and a geographical basis (though there are exemptions for some classes of company).

SSAP25 requires that, in deciding how to break the entity down into segments, regard should be had to the purpose of presenting segmented information, and, in particular, to the need for users to be informed where segments earn returns out of line with the entity's overall return or involve different degrees of risk, rates of growth or potential. This approach may be contrasted with that in the US which now (since 1997) requires that segment definitions follow the organization's internal management reporting structure. The case for this approach is that the reporting basis found most useful by management is also likely to be the most useful for users of the external financial reports. However, since the organizational structure may not reflect different degrees of profitability, risk, growth and potential, the information disclosed may be lower in quality and less comparable with that from other entities. It is unlikely that the US approach is compatible with the presentation guidelines in the Statement of Principles, though, in practice, internal organizational structure may be closely aligned with a segmental structure complying with UK GAAP in many instances.

Exceptional and extraordinary items

The presentation in the statement of financial performance of 'abnormal' items, that is items that are unusual in the context of the business and unlikely to recur with any frequency, has been a matter of controversy for many years. Prior to the adoption of SSAP6 in 1974 it was common for companies to exclude some items from the profit and loss account altogether, simply including them in the footnote showing movements in reserves. Items excluded in this way could include operating matters, such as large abnormal losses, as well as 'technical' items like differences on foreign currency translation. This approach was felt to be likely to understate the significance of some of these items and SSAP6 required that they be shown on the face of the profit and loss account but introduced the category of 'extraordinary items' so as to present them separately.

Unfortunately, in practice many companies chose to widen the classification of extraordinary items to include categories of gain and loss which occurred fairly regularly and were quite closely related to the normal operations of the business. For example, a large chain of hotels and public houses would expect to buy and sell individual outlets every year as well as continuing to operate most of the outlets it owned at the beginning of the year. Yet it might treat gains and losses on the sale of outlets as an extraordinary item, and thus have the same extraordinary item in its profit and loss account year after year. This undermines the meaning of the category and also potentially confuses users trying to assess future cash flows or earnings, who might assume, looking at one or two years' information only, that no further gain or loss would be expected in future years.

FRS3, issued in October 1992, sought to cure this abuse by emphasizing that extraordinary items were to be regarded as being 'extremely rare' (paragraph 49). It underlined this approach by widening the definition of 'ordinary activities', compared with that in SSAP6, and giving no examples of extraordinary items, presumably because they are so rare that no one on the ASB could think of even one example. The approach of FRS3 has worked: the Chairman of the ASB regards extraordinary items as having effectively been abolished (Davies et al., 1999: 1506).[1]

The result of the abolition of extraordinary items is that some really quite abnormal items are now included in the exceptional category and there may be a tendency for users to focus on the profit before exceptional items. This could be misleading, since exceptional items include some that are likely to occur fairly frequently, though not necessarily every year, and some that will recur every year but which happen to be of an unusually large size in the current year.

We can view the tension between permitting a category of genuinely very abnormal items and controlling the abuse of this category to include 'not so abnormal' items (generally debits), in the hope that users will ignore them or at least attach less significance to them than they should, as part of the struggle to achieve the most relevant presentation of information that is also reliable. Classifying recurrent items as extraordinary undermines faithful representation because the information does not then depict what it purports to depict.

Dividends paid and proposed

Current GAAP and company law require that dividends paid and proposed to be paid out of the result for the period be shown in the profit and loss account. Under the Statement of Principles' approach, however, dividends are not a loss but rather a distribution to owners. In pursuit of consistency of classification and clarity of presentation, the Statement requires that the statement of financial performance should include only gains and losses. Hence, the Statement is inconsistent with current GAAP and company law. The Statement's position is, however, logical and consistent with its own approach to the definition of financial statement elements and, particularly, the distinction between liabilities and ownership interest. Under the Statement of Principles, dividends for the period would be shown in a reconciliation of movements in ownership interest. We have already seen (Chapter 5) that proposed dividends are not a liability.

Although the treatment of dividends set out here will be unfamiliar to practising accountants and users of financial statements, it would emphasize the distinction between liabilities and ownership interest and between changes in ownership interest generated by the activities of the entity and those coming about from transactions with owners. The nature of dividends is, arguably, recognized already in current GAAP by their positioning at the very bottom of the profit and loss account.

Statutory formats

Company law requires that the profit and loss account and balance sheet be presented in formats chosen from among those prescribed in the legislation. The Statement argues that, although these formats may not be fully in compliance with the guidance set out in the Statement, inconsistencies can 'generally' (SP, Appendix I, paragraph 11) be overcome by additional disclosure. It remains the case that the 'best' presentation that could be achieved following the guidance might not be compatible with the statutory formats.

One question that the Statement of Principles does not address is whether the classification scheme in the statutory formats, which follows that traditionally used in UK GAAP, is actually consistent with its approach to element definitions. For example, the classification 'stocks' includes a subclassification for 'payments on account'. Payments on account are payments made by the entity to a supplier in advance of receiving delivery of goods. They are assets for the entity because they embody a future economic benefit in the form of either (a) receiving the goods, which can then be sold, or manufactured into a finished product, or whatever; or (b) receiving a refund of the payment in advance if the goods are not in fact delivered. The normal way in which the benefits are received is by delivery of the goods and hence the payment is appropriately classified with stock.

However, prepayments for services (such as electricity) are classified as a subcategory of debtors. Now prepayments for services are also an asset because they embody future benefits but, as with payments in advance, the normal way in which the benefits are obtained is by receipt and consumption of the services and not by a refund of the payment. Indeed, under normal circumstances, it may not be possible for the entity to forgo consumption of the services and demand a refund. To be consistent with the treatment of payments in advance, it could be argued that prepayments should not be classified as a monetary asset since: (a) they will not normally be received in cash and it may not be possible for the entity to insist on a cash receipt; and (b) the normal way in which the benefits embodied in them are received is by consumption of services. Now, of course, it is not possible to stockpile services as such and hence there is no main classification for 'access to services' on the balance sheet. This is presumably why, historically, prepayments have been lumped in with debtors. However, if a classification scheme consistent with the Statement of Principles' element definitions and presentation objectives is to be specified, it may be necessary to revisit the question, which arises also in relation to payments in advance received by the entity.

Criticisms

Although the guidance in the chapter of the Statement of Principles covering financial statement preparation offers some sound observations and practical advice, it would be possible to make much the same criticism of it as has been offered of the chapter on measurement: it does not really take us very much beyond current practice. While it is easy to see how the guidance on the content of the primary financial statements is derived from the objective of financial statement presentation, it is less easy to see why the particular aspects emphasized in the advice were chosen. For example, why is it clear that components of the statement of financial performance should be classified by a combination of function and nature, when other characteristics from the list given earlier could have been chosen? A critic might suggest that the specific guidance has been shaped by current GAAP, and particularly company law, which requires that the profit and loss account is structured in this way.

It is not clear that the Statement of Principles' notion that gross revenue is a gain and cost of sales is a loss, with the profit on the transaction being a netting of the gain and loss, corresponds to what is normally understood by gains and losses. It is, of course, open to a conceptual framework to define terms differently from their normal usage, but such differences should, at least, be emphasized. It is also unclear, however, that sales revenue satisfies the definition of an increase in ownership interest, according to the economic model adopted by the Statement, when the bookkeeping credit can be achieved only by accepting the accompanying bookkeeping debit of the cost of sales. In other words, ownership interest increases in purely bookkeeping terms when the credit entry is made, but the increase in net assets that can be achieved from the sale (and thus the increase in ownership interest viewed in terms of economic substance) is limited to the profit.

Notes

1 The ASB cannot formally abolish extraordinary items since they are a classification within the statutory formats for the profit and loss account.

References

Davies, M., Paterson, R. and Wilson, A. (1999) UK GAAP, 6th edn. London: Macmillan.

Further reading

For a discussion of the development of GAAP relating to segmental reporting and extraordinary items, see M. Davies, R. Paterson and A. Wilson, *UK GAAP*, 6th edn, London: Macmillan, 1999, Chapters 19 and 22.

10

The Reporting Entity

Until this point we have taken it for granted that we know the answer to two questions: (a) which entities should produce financial statements; and (b) how do we decide what constitutes an individual entity for the purpose of determining the scope of a set of financial statements? The Statement of Principles uses the term *reporting entity* to describe an entity for which financial statements should be produced, so that these two questions become: (a) what entities are reporting entities; and (b) how should we define the boundaries of a reporting entity?

The Statement of Principles examines these questions quite early on – in fact in its second chapter. However, the answer to the second question is actually rather complex and the Statement has to take a second bite at it after the rest of the framework has been established. The answers to the two questions do not affect our understanding of the remainder of the framework so it has been convenient to defer consideration of them until now.

The entities that should produce financial statements

According to the Statement of Principles:

> An entity should prepare and publish financial statements if there is a legitimate demand for the information that its financial statements would provide and it is a cohesive economic unit. (SP, p. 26)

The argument that financial statements should be produced where there is a legitimate demand for them follows from the user needs perspective. It should be noted, however, that the Statement of Principles is largely silent on what constitutes a 'legitimate' demand, acknowledging that it is leaving this essentially political question for others to resolve (SP, Appendix III, paragraph 14). The Statement does, however, indicate that in any particular case the benefit flowing from the production of financial statements should exceed their cost of production.

The Statement of Principles argues that the information provided by the financial statements will only be useful if the entity that is the subject of those statements, that is, the reporting entity, is a 'cohesive economic unit' (SP, 2.3). What constitutes a cohesive economic unit is determined by the ability to control activities. This achieves two things. First, it provides accountability because the financial statements focus on those activities over which the reporting entity has control, and for which it can reasonably be held accountable. Secondly, as we shall see, it provides a clear rationale for drawing the boundary between a reporting entity and the rest of the world.

The boundary of the reporting entity

The business world is composed of individual, organizationally and legally separate, units (for example, companies), undertaking transactions and experiencing other events. The scope of the financial statements of a reporting entity is determined by: (a) the way in which those individual units are grouped together to form a single reporting entity; and (b) which of the particular transactions and other events experienced by those units are selected for inclusion in the statements.

The key to the approach adopted by the Statement of Principles in both cases is *control*. For the reporting entity to be in a position to exercise control over activities it is necessary, according to the Statement of Principles, that it has the ability to both:

1   deploy the economic resources involved, and
2   receive the benefits (or suffer the losses) that result from their deployment.

In some cases, for example trusteeship, the ability to deploy resources and the ability to benefit from their deployment are held by different parties (in the case of a trust, the trustees deploy the resources and the beneficiaries enjoy the result) and hence control, in the sense in which the term is used here, does not exist.

We have already seen (Chapters 4–6) how the concept of control works in determining how transactions and other events fall within the scope of the financial statements by the part it plays in the definition of assets, and hence liabilities, gains and losses. We can now examine how control works in determining how separate business units are grouped together to form reporting entities.

The constitutional structure of the business sector

This is not a work on business law. For our purposes, we can think of the business sector as composed of a large number of individual units, predominantly companies, partnerships and sole proprietorships, but also with a variety of more exotic species, such as charter corporations. Each of these has an organizationally or legally separate existence and, in most cases, the units are *both* legally and organizationally separate from other units. However, although they remain legally separate, one unit can own another, or have some other relationship which gives the former power over the latter: classically, one company can own some or all of the shares in another. In straightforward circumstances a company which owns more than 50% of the shares in another can control the latter by exercising its votes (or, more commonly, by threatening to do so) in a general meeting of shareholders, the ultimate governing body of the company. In this case the company owning the shares is the *parent* and the company whose shares are owned is the *subsidiary*.

Single entity and group financial statements

The Statement of Principles establishes two types of control, which yield different concepts of reporting entity and different categories of financial statement. *Direct control* is control exercised by an entity directly over activities and resources. Applying the test of direct control yields a reporting entity which produces *single entity financial statements,* covering only the assets and liabilities it controls or bears directly. If it controls other entities, it will do so by having direct control over the instruments which embody that control and these instruments may represent assets (as is the case, for example, where control over another company is exercised by means of ownership of shares). The control it has over the other entity will feature in its single entity financial statements by the inclusion of the assets and liabilities that are associated with its control over the other entity (such as shares), rather than by the inclusion of the other entity as such. Consequently, where one entity controls another, its single entity financial statements focus on the other entity as an investment and on its generation of income, rather than on its business operations and the assets and liabilities it controls.

By contrast, *indirect control* is control exercised by one entity over another entity's assets and liabilities by means of the first entity's control over the second entity itself. Applying both tests of control – direct and indirect – together yields a reporting entity which produces *group* or *consolidated financial statements,* covering all the assets and liabilities controlled or borne, directly or indirectly, by a parent. The reporting entity is the group (that is, the parent and all its subsidiaries) and the financial statements aggregate the assets, liabilities, gains, losses and cash flows of the parent and its subsidiaries. The assets owned by the parent, which represent the means by which control is exercised over its subsidiaries, must be excluded from these statements, in order to avoid double counting by including both the assets which represent the means of control and the assets over which that control is exercised.

Because the central notion here is one of control, all the assets, liabilities, gains, losses and cash flows are brought into the financial statements: all the assets are controlled by the parent, even when the parent does not own the whole of the subsidiary. The proportion of the ownership interest in a subsidiary not held by the parent is accounted for separately to reveal the extent of the parent's 'access and exposure to the results of its subsidiaries' (SP, 8.12).

Single entity financial statements are of limited usefulness when the entity is part of a larger group and the Statement of Principles accepts this (SP, Appendix III, paragraphs 18–19). This is because the reporting entity effectively controls a wider range of assets than appears in its single entity financial statements and can use this control to influence the content of its single entity financial statements by the way it interacts with the remainder of the group. Some commentators would argue that it is, indeed, no longer appropriate to require the production of single entity financial statements under these circumstances. However, the Statement of Principles argues that they do have some role to play.

The nature of control over another entity

The Statement of Principles enlarges on its definition of control in the context of entities (by contrast with assets) by saying that:

> An entity will have control of a second entity if it has the ability to direct that entity's operating and financial policies with a view to gaining economic benefit from its activities. (SP, 2.11)

The Statement of Principles goes on to discuss the application of this test in a number of cases; an examination of these cases is outside the scope of this text.[1]

Joint control and influence

A reporting entity may have an interest in another entity (for example owing some of its shares) which stops short of giving it control over that entity (and thus does not give it indirect control over its assets). The Statement of Principles distinguishes three cases (SP, 8.4):

1 joint control, that is control as previously defined exercised only with one or more other parties
2 significant influence over operating and financial policies (and hence deployment of economic resources and the enjoyment of benefits)
3 little or no influence.

Consolidated financial statements need to reflect assets and liabilities over which the reporting entity has joint control or significant influence (because users will find information about them useful) but must not do so in a way that implies that they are controlled by the reporting entity. The methods to be employed to achieve this lie outside the scope of this text.[2]

Notes

1 Consideration of the nature of control over another entity in this level of detail is best examined as part of coverage of group accounting.

2 Again, these are best dealt with in the course of studying group accounting.

Further reading

For a discussion of the issues that arise in producing consolidated financial statements, see P. Taylor, *Consolidated Financial Reporting*, London: Paul Chapman, 1996; and M. Davies, R. Paterson and A. Wilson, *UK GAAP*, 6th edn, London: Macmillan, 1999.

Index